THE BIRTH OF MODERN EUROPE

Trevor Cairns

ART EDITORS BANKS AND MILES

CAMBRIDGE UNIVERSITY PRESS

Paintings and drawings by
Anna Mieke
Maps by Reg Piggott
Diagrams by Banks and Miles

Published by the Syndics of the Cambridge University Press
Bentley House, 200 Euston Road, London NW1 2DB
American Branch: 32 East 57th Street, New York, N.Y.10022

© Cambridge University Press 1975

First published 1975

Library of Congress Catalogue Card Number: 74–111127
ISBN 0 521 07728 1

Printed and bound in Great Britain by
Jarrold and Sons Ltd, Norwich

front cover: Contemporary bronze medallion of a man of the Renaissance, Leon Battista Alberti (see page 38). The diameter of the medallion is 3⅝ ins. (9·2 cm).

back cover: An imperial hunting party in the Tyrol, about 1504 (see page 49).

Contents

In 1636 Cardinal Richelieu, in Paris, wanted a bust made by the famous sculptor Bernini, in Rome. So the painter Philippe de Champaigne produced a portrait to show the cardinal's features completely to the sculptor.

Periods, people and portraits

When did the Modern World begin?

There could be many good answers to that question. Here is one of the best-known.

Historians often break up history into three main periods: ancient, medieval, modern. If we follow this idea, it means that such decisive changes took place in western Europe round about the year 1500 that they fixed the main outlines of the world we know today.

There is no doubt that very important things were happening. The kingdoms of Europe grew into states with strong governments; often they were the same nation-states that you see on today's map. These strong governments began to keep in touch with one another all the time, by means of ambassadors who lived at one another's courts; it was the start of modern diplomacy, which we still have to rely upon to keep peace between the nations. These are only two of the big developments. There were new ideas on everything from manners to the shape of the universe. The medieval Church split; instead of one Church for the whole of western Christendom there arose several Christian religions, each with its own ideas about God, about what God expected and about how people should behave.

Britain shared in all these developments. But, perhaps because of the seas which parted her from the rest of Europe, there were some interesting differences as well.

In some ways, of course, every century and every period has done something to build up the world you live in, and so to make you the person that you are. Yet while we remember this, and wonder if it is sensible to think of any one time as *the* beginning of our own world, we still have to admit that the period of the Renaissance (as we call the time covered in this book) was very important to us.

When we talked about *a period* having *done* something we were not being accurate. A period cannot do anything. What we meant was that *the people alive during the period* did it. In this book you will see many people whose deeds have in some ways affected your life.

You will see them, but not only with your own eyes. You will be using the sharp eyes of artists, too. The Renaissance was a period when art of all kinds made great progress, and so we have portraits of most of the leading people who lived then. See what you think of them. We all spend a lot of time studying other people; for example, that is what we are doing when we watch a play, a film, television. Even if we never think of it as study, all the time we are judging them, deciding if we like them, or trust them, or want them to succeed.

How often do you judge someone by his face, by the look in his eyes or the way his mouth is set? Is this a good way of judging, or are there better methods?

At any rate, the portraits in this book will show you what those famous people looked like, and it is up to you to decide if this helps you to form an opinion about them. Judge for yourself – but be fair, be careful, and remember that there is a difference between knowing the truth and knowing the whole truth.

4

1. RENAISSANCE EUROPE

The Tudor monarchy in England

Hero or villain?

This is probably the best-known face in English history. Everybody knows Henry VIII, the king who was married six times. Most people also know that he quarrelled with the Pope, and separated the Church of England from the Catholic Church.

Nobody questions the facts, but there are fierce arguments about *why* he did such things, and about what sort of a man he was. Some writers have described him as selfish, cruel, evil: 'a blot of blood and grease upon the History of England', as Charles Dickens put it. Others have preferred to think of him as 'Bluff King Hal', the monarch who enjoyed life, was the idol of his people, and built up England into a proud state, ready and able to smash any attempt by larger states to interfere with her freedom.

Tyrant or patriot – what was this man?

In 1537 Henry VIII and his third wife, Jane Seymour, were painted by Hans Holbein. The king's portrait was much admired, and several copies were made – fortunately, for the original was destroyed in 1698 when the palace of Whitehall was burnt down.

The inheritance

Henry VIII was just under eighteen when he became king. For hundreds of years – perhaps since the Norman Conquest – no king of England had begun his reign with so much in his favour. He had great riches, loyal and clever servants, an obedient people, and no rival claimants to his throne. He owed all this to his father, Henry VII, the man who had founded the Tudor royal family. We need to understand the work of Henry VII before we can begin to judge Henry VIII.

Henry VII had become king the hard way.

In the middle of the fifteenth century England had been plagued by civil wars, which historians have named the Wars of the Roses. Two branches of the English royal family, the House of York and the House of Lancaster, fought for the crown. It was a savage fight. Each side, when it won a battle, executed as many of the leaders of the other side as it could catch.

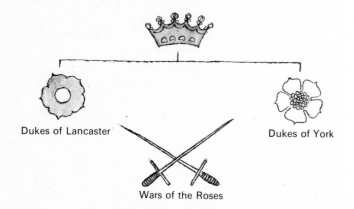

Dukes of Lancaster

Dukes of York

Wars of the Roses

In 1485 Henry Tudor, grandson of a Welsh squire, was chief of the House of Lancaster, because all the Lancastrians with better claims had been killed. He was living in exile in France while the Yorkist king, Richard III, ruled England. Richard made many enemies who decided to help Henry. Henry landed in Wales, marched into England, and defeated and killed Richard at Bosworth, near Leicester.

Now that he had the crown, his task was to keep it, and to make sure that his children would inherit it after him. In solving his problems he created the state which Henry VIII was to inherit.

FIRST, THERE MUST BE NO OTHER CHOICE. Nobody else must have a reasonable claim to the throne. Henry married Princess Elizabeth of York, so that their children would unite both the Yorkist and the Lancastrian claims to the crown. When their first son, their heir, was born, Henry named him Arthur. This was a name which had not been used by either the Lancastrian or the Yorkist family, and it reminded people of the ancient hero-king of Britain.

Henry VII

Elizabeth of York

Arthur

There had been so much killing in the wars that hardly anybody was left who could claim to be rightful heir to the throne. Of the few who could, Henry managed to kill or capture almost every one. Discontented Yorkist barons twice found young men whom they persuaded to pretend to be Yorkist princes. The first, Lambert Simnel, was only a boy; Henry captured him, pardoned him and gave him a job in the palace kitchen. The second, Perkin Warbeck, was much more of a nuisance, and at last Henry had to have him hanged. 'Had to', because Henry VII never shed blood unless he felt that there was no other way of solving a problem. Perhaps he thought that this would show everybody how much times had changed.

SECOND, THERE MUST BE NO POWERFUL TROUBLE-MAKERS. During the Middle Ages kings had very often been prevented from having their own way by the Church or the barons. By now, in most parts of Europe, the Church gave the kings no more trouble; the king managed to control the elections of bishops, and he took care to see that nobody dangerous became a bishop. This was as true in England as in other parts of Europe. But the nobles were still a menace.

During the wars the richer nobles had collected gangs of servants, 'retainers'. These men often carried weapons, and wore the badge or uniform of their master; 'livery' was the name for such a badge or clothes. The gangs were sometimes big enough to be private armies. A baron with a force like this could rule over a whole district, and anyone who stood up against him would be made to suffer. The king's judges had often been unable to interfere. Even if the judges themselves were honest and brave enough to do their duty, witnesses could always be got at. So the barons had been able to 'maintain' their retainers in the courts. During the Wars of the Roses no king had been strong enough to stop it. The nobles seemed more of a problem than ever.

In fact, Henry VII was lucky. The barons and their retainers had killed one another so enthusiastically during the wars that many noble families had been badly weakened. And if, for example, the heir or heiress to a great estate was still a child, the guardian was likely to be none other than the king himself. So Henry did not find it too difficult to make and enforce laws against livery and maintenance. If a noble broke those laws, he would be summoned before a part of the King's Council, called the Court of Star Chamber because it met in a room decorated with stars, and would probably be sentenced to pay a really heavy fine.

Richard Beauchamp, earl of Warwick, shown riding back from an embassy in 1419 and reporting to the king. While the earl wears his coat of arms, his men display his livery badge, which is quite different: the bear and ragged staff, or the ragged staff only. The drawing comes from a book made about 1485 and shows costume and armour of this later date.

The great nobles had always thought themselves entitled to sit on the King's Council, but Henry had other ideas. He did not want on his Council anybody who might be strong enough to cause trouble. Nobles were simply not invited.

ROYAL COUNCIL BARONS KEEP OUT

THIRD, THERE MUST BE SUPPORT FROM THE MOST USEFUL PEOPLE. The men Henry did want were those with brains and education; with money and influence, too, as long as they did not have enough to be dangerous. This meant the people just below the barons, people who were glad to see the great lords cut down to size. These men were mainly country gentlemen, knights and squires; or merchants from the thriving towns – for, in spite of the wars, trade had been rich; or lawyers, who were often connected with the other two classes. Altogether, we can call these people, loosely, the middle classes. They were sure to support any king who looked as if he could give them peace, order and justice after the long years of disorder and uncertainty. (We may guess that most Englishmen, including some of the nobles themselves, felt the same way.) So Henry VII had an advantage, and when he began to use the middle classes as his trusted agents, they were with him solidly.

The king used clever men of this sort on his Council, which soon became known as the Privy (or secret) Council. Sometimes these councillors sat in special courts, which were branches of the Privy Council. The most famous was the Court of Star Chamber, which, as you have seen, stamped on disorderly barons, but could turn its attention to any sort of case. There was the Court of Requests, specially interested in the pleas of poor men who could not afford the lawyers' fees in ordinary courts. There were branches of the Council which sat in remote and warlike parts of the country: the Councils of the North, of the West, of the Marches of Wales.

How the Tudor monarch used the middle classes to help them in governing: the centre of power was the crown, and all authority radiated from it;

attending upon the monarch, or sitting regularly at Westminster, were the Privy Council and some of its branches;

in distant areas where trouble might break out other branches of the Council were set up;

in every county the leading local gentlemen acted as magistrates, and generally carried out the orders of the king and Council.

All over the country men of the middle classes served the king as Justices of the Peace. It was their duty to enforce in their districts anything that the king and Council wanted. They held courts to try small offences, they sometimes fixed the maximum prices at which goods could be sold and the maximum wages which workmen could be paid, they dealt with the unemployed and the beggars, they recruited soldiers when there was need for them. J.P.s served without pay (as most of them still do nowadays) and they were glad to do so; partly because they wanted to help to keep order and peace, partly because being a J.P. made them more important in their own districts.

All these courts and jobs were not invented by Henry VII himself. Often he was using ideas which earlier kings had tried, or giving a new importance to an old office, like that of J.P. Sometimes one of the institutions we have mentioned – the Council of the North, for example – was not working properly until many years after his death. All the same, it is fair to think of Henry VII as the king who really decided that England was going to be governed according to this new pattern.

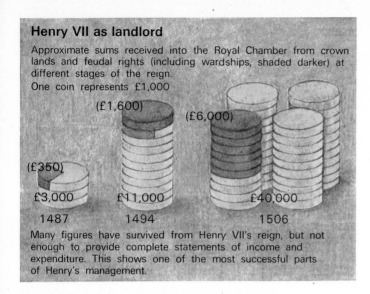

Henry VII as landlord

Approximate sums received into the Royal Chamber from crown lands and feudal rights (including wardships, shaded darker) at different stages of the reign.
One coin represents £1,000

(£350)

(£1,600)

(£6,000)

£3,000   £11,000   £40,000
1487   1494   1506

Many figures have survived from Henry VII's reign, but not enough to provide complete statements of income and expenditure. This shows one of the most successful parts of Henry's management.

right: Yeoman warder and yeoman clerk at the Tower of London. Their full-dress uniform has changed little in over four centuries.

FOURTH, THERE MUST BE MONEY AND ARMED FORCE. Probably every ruler in history has known the importance of these two; they are the most obvious ways of being powerful. Henry VII was far from being the first to have a great interest in money, and he may not even have invented any new ways of raising it. Yet he has been called the best business man who ever sat on the English throne. The royal estates were large, especially because of the lands which had been con-fiscated during the Wars of the Roses; the income from the king's lands rose from £13,000 at the beginning of his reign to £32,000 after twenty years of his good management. As you saw on page 7, he punished offenders by fines. He did all he could to help merchants, for the more goods flowed through the ports, the more he got in customs dues. He made very advantageous trade treaties with the wealthy Low Countries, and even hired out the royal ships to go on trading voyages. He got money from his Parliament in order to fight the king of France, and then accepted money from the king of France to stop the war. He encouraged people to make him presents – 'benevolences' they were called, which means kindnesses; it was understood that the king was more likely to be kind to people who had been kind to him. Early in his

reign he was short of money, and had to borrow; but, unlike many kings, he was careful to repay properly, so that in future he would be trusted if he needed to borrow again. From 1492 onwards, he was collecting more than he was spending every year. He used every means to get money, and his tax-gatherers were especially unpopular. He used his surplus to lend to merchants and foreign princes, and to buy jewels and gold plate worth about £250,000 in the money of those days.

When all else fails, a government has to rely on force. Many kings have tried to keep a powerful army. Henry VII did not. He relied upon being clever enough most of the time not to need an army, and having enough foresight to see when danger threatened and enough money to raise troops to meet it. Meanwhile, as armies were terribly expensive, he would save his money until it was really needed. There were only two exceptions.

Cannon were hard to buy in a hurry, and hard to make, so he kept a train of artillery in the Tower of London. Nobody else was allowed to have such big guns. To protect him against murder plots he founded the Yeomen of the Guard, the Beef-eaters, as his personal escort. Unlike the retainers of barons, they wore uniform, the royal Tudor livery.

By the time he had done all these things, Henry VII had made the king of England very definitely master in his kingdom. We can represent his way of governing in a diagram, and you see how all the power seems to come from the king himself. This system of government has been called the Tudor Despotism, for a despot is a ruler who has all the power in his own hands. Some historians, though, do not like the name, because they think that a real despot would not have had to depend so much on the support of the middle classes as the Tudor monarchs did.

COUNCILLORS

J.P.s

ordinary people

One thing is missing from the diagram: Parliament. It still existed and, as you saw on page 9, Henry sometimes found it useful. Usually he did not bother to call it, and when he did he could be sure that it would do as he wished. He could depend on the bishops in the House of Lords, and in the Commons the M.P.s were men of the middle classes, men who realised that the king wanted the same things as they did, that they were on the same side.

Other kings in other countries of Europe were doing rather similar things at about the same time, making themselves masters of their states in a way that no medieval king had been. Historians have called these 'the new monarchs'.

FIFTH, THERE MUST BE FOREIGN FRIENDS. Henry wanted to marry his children to other princes and princesses. This was partly to make sure that the foreign kings would not support any Yorkist adventurer who tried to attack him – Perkin Warbeck had got help from the Low Countries and Scotland – but mainly to prove that the Tudors really had 'arrived' and that other kings thought their friendship worth having.

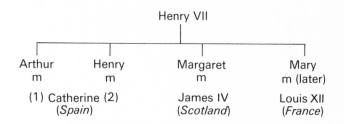

Henry VII

Arthur m	Henry m	Margaret m	Mary m (later)
(1) Catherine (2) (*Spain*)		James IV (*Scotland*)	Louis XII (*France*)

The map and the family diagram show what happened. For his son Arthur there was a Spanish princess, Catherine of Aragon. Henry saw that Spain was becoming a strong state, and he also thought that the marriage would make a link with the Low Countries, where Catherine's sister was the wife of the ruler. Catherine's father, King Ferdinand, was another 'new monarch', just as clever as Henry himself. If Ferdinand thought it wise to intermarry with the Tudors, then the Tudors must be important.

As it happened, Arthur died young. But Henry VII kept Catherine (and her dowry) in England, and promised that she should marry his second son, also called Henry, the boy who was to become Henry VIII.

The other important marriage was that of Princess Margaret to King James IV of Scotland. When some of his advisers were worried because, some day in the future, this might lead to England being joined to Scotland under a Scottish king, Henry VII merely said that 'the greater would draw the less'. Whatever the nationality of the king, he meant, Scotland was too small to be the leading partner.

England and her neighbours
in the later part of the reign of Henry VII

England
France
Scotland
Spain
Habsburg lands
Boundary of Holy Roman Empire

Henry VII died in 1509. He has been called the ablest of the Tudors, and they were a very able family. Francis Bacon called him 'a wonder for wise men'. Does this face fit your ideas about him?

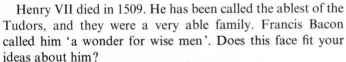
Two views of Henry VII. The portrait was painted by M. Sittow in 1505, when the king was 48. Below is his death mask; the nose is restored, otherwise it has remained unaltered since 1509.

Renaissance prince

The new king was like a story-book prince. He was gay, friendly, handsome. He loved sports – hunting, wrestling, tennis, jousting – and was good at all of them. He wrote poetry and composed and played music. He began his reign romantically, too. The old king, Henry VII, had kept putting off the marriage between young Henry and Catherine of Aragon, in order to try to gain advantages over Ferdinand. The young king swept aside all this diplomacy and politics, and married his Spanish princess.

In Renaissance times many kings and princes tried to be splendid figures, but none was more splendid than Henry VIII. There was more in this than just showing off and spending money, though. A good Renaissance prince ought to have a mind to match his appearance. He should be wise, clever, educated, cultivated; a friend of scholars and artists. Henry VIII was a Renaissance prince in these respects, too. He had been particularly carefully educated, because while his brother Arthur had still been alive there had been an idea that Henry might enter the Church, perhaps to become archbishop of Canterbury; so Henry had been given an education which would have fitted him for such a job. In 1520 he was able to write a book against Martin Luther, the German monk who had defied the Pope. Henry was rewarded by the Pope with the title of 'Fidei Defensor' (Defender of the Faith), which is still among the royal titles on British coins.

Learned men were welcome at Henry's court. One famous visitor to England was the Dutchman Erasmus, who was admired even by other scholars for his skill in writing in Latin and Greek, and for his witty satires on the silly and ignorant behaviour of many priests and monks. An English scholar whom Henry treated as a friend was Thomas More, the brilliant lawyer who wrote *Utopia*.

The famous German artist Hans Holbein also visited England. You may have noticed that most of the good portraits of Henry and his courtiers were painted by Holbein.

right: A tennis court in a palace garden; detail from an engraving of a German painting, early sixteenth century.

Erasmus was an internationally famed scholar in his late fifties when Hans Holbein painted his portrait (*far left*) in 1523. It was in 1543, the year of his death at the age of 45, that Holbein painted the miniature of himself (*left*).

Henry VIII; born 1491, king 1509, died 1547.

A great prince, of course, had to be glorious in war, and Henry took special interest in guns and ships. His famous battleship, *Henri Grâce à Dieu* (nicknamed 'Great Harry'), had scores of little man-killing guns in its high 'castles' and its batteries of heavy ship-killing guns lower down. Near the end of his reign Henry built a series of new-style castles along the south coast, specially designed for use with big guns against attacks from over the Channel.

So Henry VIII played the part of a splendid, powerful, highly civilised monarch. Here is the full portrait, of which you saw only the face on page 5. The costume and the way he is standing may tell you something more about him.

The picture of Henry VIII's embarkation at Dover was probably painted many years afterwards, and anyway the proportions are obviously faulty. But it conveys many ideas clearly — the new circular artillery forts, the towering build of the warships, and above all, the splendid show of a Tudor 'royal occasion'.

And what did this splendid king achieve?

He left the dull work, the day-to-day running of his kingdom, to his servants. He could do this because his father had left things running so smoothly, and had trained such very good servants. The most famous of the men on whom Henry VIII relied was Thomas Wolsey, a churchman. He served the king so well that he became abbot of St Albans, bishop of Durham, archbishop of York, and cardinal with special powers from the Pope. (The Pope was usually willing to confer honours when a king requested.) One of Wolsey's main tasks was to provide money, for Henry VIII, as you must have realised, soon went through his father's savings and was always needing more.

Between them, the king and his cardinal made a great show among the princes of Europe. They made alliances, declared war, fought and won battles, attended conferences and signed treaties. It was all very spectacular and very expensive. And the profit, after twenty years, was: *nil*.

The work of Henry and Wolsey is summed up in Henry's visit to France, to meet King Francis I for a fortnight in June 1520. It was so dazzling and costly that the meeting-place near Calais was called 'The Field of Cloth of Gold'. Both kings spent fortunes on entertaining each other, and swore friendship, and it was all a complete sham. Henry sailed home and immediately made an alliance with the Emperor Charles V, the enemy of Francis. England gained nothing from that alliance, either.

Master of Church and state

It is easy enough for us, looking back, to see that Henry's effort to be the strong man of Europe was an expensive flop. It was not so easy for Henry to see it, for he lived magnificently and was surrounded by people who tried to please him. There was, however, one big failure which nobody could conceal from him; he had not been able to get a legitimate son. Catherine of Aragon had given him only a daughter, Mary. It was this failure which led to the really important events in Henry VIII's reign.

Henry decided that he must be rid of his wife. He had a political motive: it would be dangerous to leave the kingdom to a girl because, as most people then believed, ruling a kingdom needed the full strength of a man. He had a religious motive: Catherine had been married to Arthur, and it was against God's law to marry your brother's widow. True, the Pope had given special permission. But perhaps this was not enough, and God was punishing Henry and Catherine by not letting them have a boy. He also had a personal motive. Her name was Anne Bullen, or Boleyn.

Historians have argued about which of these motives was the strongest. It is almost impossible to say, because they were all urging Henry in the same direction.

Henry thought that he would be able to persuade the Pope easily to do as he wanted, to declare that there had been a mistake and that Henry and Catherine had never been properly married. But this is where the trouble started. The Pope hedged. Catherine was the aunt of the Emperor Charles, and the Pope was even less willing to offend the emperor than the king of England. Months slipped by, then years. Henry became furious. Wolsey failed to persuade the Pope, so the king sent him off to York, in disgrace, to spend his time on

Thomas Wolsey, 1475(?)–1530. The artist and date of this portrait are unknown, but it is probably a good likeness of the cardinal.

his Church duties. While Wolsey was away from Court, the king became even more furious when he thought of the way the cardinal had failed him. So Henry called Wolsey back, and would have had him tried and executed for treason if the cardinal had not died on his journey to London

Henry next tried to put real pressure on the Pope. He called Parliament, and at the government's suggestion they began to pass acts against the Pope, little ones, gradually cutting down the fees and offerings which went from England to the Papal treasury in Rome. (Henry was cunning. If the Pope were to give way, and Henry were to become his devoted friend once more, it would be possible to put all the blame for these acts on to Parliament.) The Pope tried to please Henry in most things, even appointing one of Henry's supporters, Thomas Cranmer, as the new archbishop of Canterbury; but he would not give way on the one point which Henry really wanted, annulling the marriage.

So Henry took his big decision. Remember that he had been educated to know a great deal about Church matters. He felt no doubt that he was right, and the Pope was wrong. In 1535 he had Parliament declare that the king was Supreme Head of the Church in England. Already, two years earlier, Archbishop Cranmer had married Henry to Anne Boleyn, who thus became queen instead of Catherine of Aragon. Catherine was sent to live quietly in the country, and died in 1536.

Henry's Act of Supremacy broke a link with Rome that had lasted a thousand years. England now was going to have a Church of her own, instead of belonging to the great Church of western Christendom. Henry, however, did not see it that way. He claimed that he was not changing religion, that he was right and the Pope was wrong, that he was only correcting errors. Though he did approve of putting into the churches English translations of the Bible, chained to reading-desks so that anyone could use them, Henry would have nothing to do with the 'Protestants' who followed Martin Luther. Henry still thought as badly of Luther as when he had written his book (page 12), still thought Lutherans were wicked heretics, and went on having them burnt at the stake.

As for any Catholic who remained loyal to the Pope, he was treated not as a heretic, but as a traitor. The punishment was either beheading or hanging, drawing and quartering. Nobody was spared. Henry's 'friend', Thomas More, who had been made chancellor in place of Wolsey, could not agree and tried to retire quietly. This was not allowed. He was ordered to swear obedience to the king's religious ideas, and, when he would not do so, he was beheaded.

The death of a Protestant writer during the reign of Henry VIII's Catholic daughter Mary. From a Protestant propaganda book, John Foxe's *Book of Martyrs*, this edition printed in 1554.

The death of Catholic monks during the reign of Henry VIII. From a Catholic propaganda book printed in 1587, when Queen Elizabeth had renewed such executions.

Thomas More was one of the very few who stood out against what the king did. Yet this was an enormous change, which made the king supreme in Church as well as state, in religion as well as politics. Why was there so little protest? It may well have been that few people realised how big the change was, because the church services went on with very little alteration. As for the ordinary people, most of them were used to doing what they were told, and they believed – you see this in the Robin Hood legends, for instance – that a genuine king was always good and trustworthy. The middle classes, as you know, were on the king's side anyway,

Thomas Cromwell, 1485(?)–1540. A portrait in the style of Holbein. The date is not known, but it was obviously during the years of Cromwell's power.

and many of them seem to have lost their respect for the Church long before Henry took over. They seem to have thought churchmen lazy, slack, old-fashioned; and maybe it would be easier to make money if there were fewer holy-days. The nobles of the old families may have disapproved of the king's ideas, but there was no leader among them. This may seem cowardly, but you can hardly blame anyone else when you learn that the bishops themselves gave in meekly. Only one of them, John Fisher, bishop of the rather small see of Rochester, had the courage to oppose the king. He was executed.

Serious trouble only broke out when Henry did something further. With the help of his new chief adviser, Thomas Cromwell, who had sharpened his mind by studying in Renaissance Italy and then working for Wolsey, Henry confiscated the monasteries, nunneries and friaries. He took the smaller ones in 1536, the larger in 1539. The reason he gave was that they were slack, not doing their job properly. Henry's true reason was that he wanted the wealth of the monasteries, the lands and the precious ornaments which had been given during the past five or six centuries by countless thousands of men and women, often pilgrims, who wished the monks to pray for them.

If the monks went quietly they were given other jobs or pensions. If they resisted, they were just turned out. Really troublesome ones were executed.

This Dissolution of the Monasteries was something which made a real difference, especially in the poorer parts of the country. In these parts the people more often needed the help of the monks, and anyway they tended to be more ready to fight. In the north, especially in Yorkshire, men took their bows and bills and iron caps from the wall, and began to move south. This rising is known as the Pilgrimage of Grace, and it took place in 1536. There was no standing royal army, and the king could send only a weak force to stop the thousands of warlike 'pilgrims'. But the English people trusted their king. Most of the rebels thought the Dissolution of the Monasteries was the fault of Thomas Cromwell, and that all they needed to do was to make sure that the king heard the truth; then he would put everything right. So when the king promised to investigate their complaints and not to punish anybody, they agreed to go home. They should have known better. When there was no longer any danger, the king sent his men these orders: 'You must cause such dreadful execution upon a good

Much Wenlock Priory, Shropshire; air view from the south-west. The thirteenth-century church is a ruin, and little remains of the buildings which enclosed the cloister. The infirmary and the prior's lodging, however, forming a court just to the east of the cloister, were converted into a pleasant house after the Dissolution of the Monasteries.

Few really rich church treasures seem to have survived the English Reformation. The chalice and paten, dating from the late fifteenth century, are merely of silver, parcel-gilt, and were never jewelled.

number of the inhabitants, hanging them on trees, quartering them, and setting the quarters in every town, as shall be a fearful warning.' And so it was done.

In spite of all his efforts and success, though, the king did not get as much benefit as he should have done from the wealth he had taken from the monasteries. It should have made him the richest king in Europe, if he could have kept it, but he had to spend it on armaments, such as his artillery castles. Francis I and Charles V, who were usually deadly enemies, made peace, and it looked as though they would attack England. Henry needed money so badly that he had to put many of the monastery lands on the market. The people who could afford to buy were, of course, the nobles and the middle classes, especially those working for the king, in the government and at court. Think of the number of English 'stately homes' called 'X Abbey' or 'X Priory', places which were once monasteries and were converted into houses after being bought from the king. This did help the king in one way, because the new owners would obviously try hard to prevent the return of the monks; they were bound to support the king's Church.

Poverty and roguery, as shown in Tudor wood-cuts:
From left to right:
Beggar, 1535–6.
Tom O'Bedlam (fake madman), soon after 1600.
Rogues being whipped at a cart's tail, 1567.

Did the Dissolution of the Monasteries make much difference to the ordinary people? Historians have argued about this. There is no doubt that there were many beggars, vagabonds and rogues in Tudor England, and that they were a serious problem until a workable Poor Law was made at the very end of the Tudor century. Was the problem so bad because there were no monasteries to give charity? At first sight, this may seem likely, but nobody has been able to prove that in fact the new masters were less generous than the old. One idea is that many of the beggars were peasants who had been turned off their strips of land so that the landlords could 'enclose' the old open fields for sheep-farming. It needed only a few shepherds and their dogs to look after huge flocks, on land which had supported many peasants, and there were good profits to be made from selling wool. Thomas More remarked that once men had eaten sheep, but that now sheep were eating men. Yet we cannot be certain how bad this wave of enclosures was, nor even when it really took place. Most of it may have been over before the monasteries were dissolved. Besides, it is impossible to be sure that the monks were usually kinder landlords than laymen were, especially as many monasteries had been employing business men to run their estates for them.

It is sometimes very difficult indeed, in history as in the events you read about in newspapers, to be certain of the causes and the effects of even the most famous happenings.

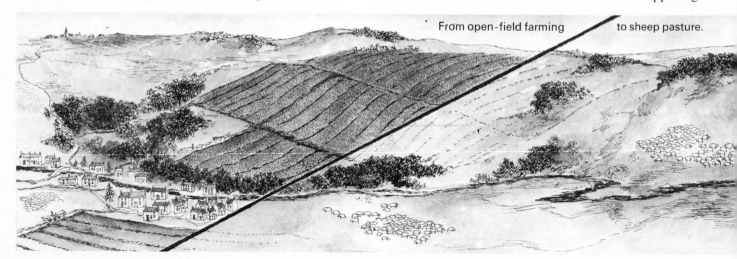

From open-field farming   to sheep pasture.

Henry VIII married:

1509 Catherine of Aragon	divorced 1533	daughter Mary b 1516
1533 Anne Boleyn	beheaded 1536	daughter Elizabeth b 1533
1536 Jane Seymour	died 1537	son Edward b 1537
1540 Anne of Cleves	divorced 1540	no issue
1540 Catherine Howard	beheaded 1542	no issue
1543 Catherine Parr	survived	no issue

We have spent time on the first two Tudor kings. One reason for this is that if you know what happened in England you will find it easier to understand the work of the other 'new monarchs', the Renaissance, the Reformation (as the great religious changes are called) and the wars which involved most of western Europe. The English story fitted in with the drama which was taking place on the main European stage.

As for Henry VIII, we must leave him with much of his story unfinished. As you see from the chart, he had many disappointments with his wives. Anne Boleyn gave him only a girl, Elizabeth, and eventually was beheaded. Only one wife gave him a son, and this was a weak, sickly child; and she died soon afterwards. Meanwhile, the king became fat. We can measure the girth of his suits of armour. He was ill, had painful ulcers on his legs, could hardly walk. Do you think that a knowledge of the king's health might help to explain some of the things he did?

Below is Henry VIII in his old age. Perhaps 'old' is a misleading word. He was only fifty-five when he died.

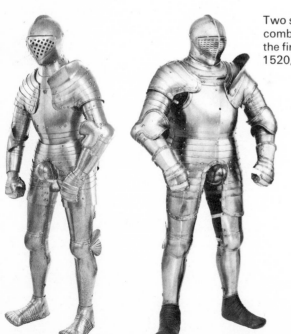

Two suits of armour for foot combat, made for Henry VIII; the first between 1515 and 1520, the second in 1540.

Henry VIII, painted by an unidentified artist about 1542.

'Nation-states' of early modern Europe

France

The map below gives some notion of the mess France was in about 1425. But sometimes (as we saw in England under Henry VII) when things are really desperate, people will allow and help the government to become stronger. So it happened in France, though not in exactly the same way as in England.

The tide of war turned, thanks partly to an astonishing peasant girl, Joan of Arc, who believed that God had told her to lead Frenchmen to victory against the hated English invaders. She did it. Eventually the English captured her and in 1431 had her burnt as a witch, but her work was done. The

Charles VII; born 1403, recognised as king in part of France 1422, crowned 1429, completed the defeat of the English 1453, died 1461. The portrait was painted by Jean Fouquet about 1451.

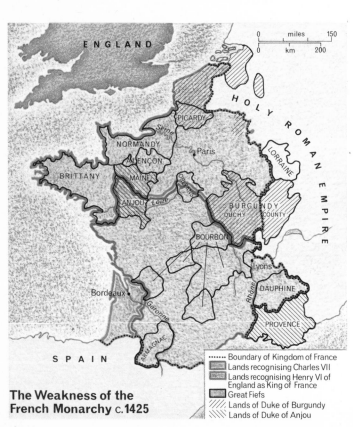

The Weakness of the French Monarchy c.1425

············ Boundary of Kingdom of France
▦ Lands recognising Charles VII
▦ Lands recognising Henry VI of England as King of France
▦ Great Fiefs
▨ Lands of Duke of Burgundy
▨ Lands of Duke of Anjou

20

This splendid mansion was built between 1436 and 1449 in Bourges by the financier Jacques Cœur. Almost as if to boast of trade, the timbers of one roof remind us of a ship's hull.

French had gained hope and strength. Joan of Arc is still the national heroine of the French.

The king she served (and who made no effort to rescue her) is known as Charles the Well Served. He had many excellent servants. Like the Tudors, he was able to pick clever men, often of the middle classes, to work for him.

Jacques Cœur, the cleverest money-man in France, took care of the finances. The Estates General (the French equivalent of the English Parliament) were so pleased to be winning the war that they allowed the king to raise a tax known as the *Taille*, which was to pay for soldiers whenever he thought it necessary, without getting the Estates' permission. Of course this meant that the king now did not need the Estates General to vote him money, and so they had less hold over him.

The king built up a professional army, which he would keep as a standing army after he had beaten the English. These were the '*gens d'armes*' (men-at-arms), the finest heavy cavalry in Europe. Each had his attendants, archers and servants, for these fully armoured cavalry needed as much servicing and supporting as a modern tank. The *gens d'armes* were traditional, the old-fashioned armoured 'knights'. There were also the latest weapons, guns for smashing walls and breaking up close-packed armies. The French king's guns were made and used by two brothers with the very middle-class name of Bureau.

Louis XI, nicknamed 'the Universal Spider', took over the task from his father, Charles, in 1461. The main problem that remained was that there were several very powerful feudal nobles, led by the duke of Burgundy, who ruled the rich Low Countries as well as Burgundy. Partly by skill, partly by luck, partly by force Louis wiped out the worst of the danger, and the kings who came afterwards finished the job.

In 1516 King Francis I made an agreement, or concordat, with the Pope, which gave him all the power he needed over the French Church. The whole fertile, rich, compact land of France was firmly under the control of the royal government.

The Strength of the French Monarchy c. **1525**

0   miles   150
0   km   200
(The dates show when the crown took control of the fiefs.)

ENGLAND

Calais

HOLY ROMAN EMPIRE

PICARDY 1477

NORMANDY 1468

Seine

Paris

ALENÇON 1458

BRITTANY 1491

MAINE 1481

ORLEANS 1498

ANJOU 1480

Loire

DUCHY OF BURGUNDY 1477

Bourges

BOURBON 1523

Lyons

Garonne

Rhône

DAUPHINE 1455

ARMAGNAC 1455

PROVENCE 1486

SPAIN

Spain

There were five separate kingdoms in the Iberian Peninsula, and one of these, Aragon, had three divisions, each with its own Cortes or Parliament. The people were independent, proud, quick to defend fiercely any of their local laws and customs when they suspected anyone of trying to break them.

When Isabella of Castile married Ferdinand of Aragon they knew that they could not make their separate peoples change to one standard set of laws and customs, and probably they did not want to, anyway. They aimed at building up the power of the Crown in Castile, which was by far the biggest and strongest kingdom.

They developed a system of Royal Councils. They employed as their councillors and as judges men of the middle classes who had been well educated. These men were known as 'letrados' or 'lettered men', and often the subject which they had studied at university was Roman law. In every big town they placed a royal officer, the 'corregidor'; unlike the Tudor J.P., the corregidor was a paid official, not a local gentleman, and he was subject to inspection regularly. It was well known that Isabella had a little black book in which she noted down the names of useful men, with the sort of jobs which she thought they would do best; she was a shrewd judge, too.

There had been bad disorder in Castile during the fifteenth century. Nobles had been able to do as they pleased, and the country had been infested by bandits. With the help of the townsmen, Ferdinand and Isabella set up a well-armed police force, the Holy Brotherhood, which had a very short way with law-breakers. They also revived the old custom of hearing and judging cases in person, especially when they thought that things might be difficult for an ordinary judge.

Isabella personally was very skilful at making the nobles respect her. They knew not only that she was strong and clever, but also that she was good and reliable. The nobles often sent their children to be brought up in the royal court, where the children grew up to have a feeling of tremendous loyalty to the queen.

One thing which all Spaniards had in common, whether they were Castilians or Aragonese, was their religion. In the south lay the kingdom of Granada, which was what remained of the once mighty caliphate of Cordoba after centuries of

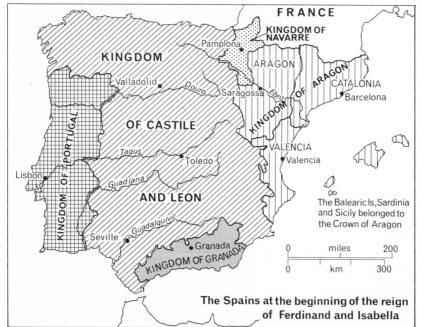

The Spains at the beginning of the reign of Ferdinand and Isabella

The Balearic Is, Sardinia and Sicily belonged to the Crown of Aragon

war between Christians and Muslims in Spain. War broke out again, and after a tough struggle Granada surrendered to Ferdinand and Isabella in 1492. Spaniards hailed it as the victorious conclusion of their *Reconquista*, their Crusade to reconquer the Peninsula from the Muslims, which had lasted 700 years.

Meanwhile, to strengthen this religious enthusiasm, Ferdinand and Isabella began the Spanish Inquisition. We shall discuss this later. All we need say now is that it was a very efficient religious secret police, controlled not by the Pope and bishops but by the king and queen and their Council.

As the coat of arms shows, the old divisions remained and this land was more complicated than other 'new monarchies'. Nevertheless, there was the same concentration of power at the top. The monarchy held, with a loyal Church to help it, the Spains together.

above right: This carving in Toledo Cathedral was made about 1495. Though damaged, it represents vividly some of the means that the Spaniards employed in attacking Granadan strongholds.

right: The triumphant entry of Ferdinand and Isabella into Granada, 1492, one of a series of coloured wood-carvings made thirty years later in the Royal Chapel, Granada. In 1494 the Pope gave them the title 'the Catholic Kings', assuming that they would carry their religion onwards into Africa and into the lands Columbus had reached.

left: The arms of the Catholic kings, from a history of Spain printed in 1493. Ferdinand (born 1452, king of Aragon 1479, died 1516) contributed the striped arms of Aragon and Sicily. Isabella (born 1451, queen of Castile 1474, died 1504) contributed the castle and lion of Castile and Leon. Together they added the pomegranate of Granada. All the Spains are under the one crown, and are held by the eagle of St John the Evangelist (which carries the Gospel far and wide). The arrows are the personal badge of Isabella. The yoke and the motto 'Tanto Monta' ('It's all the same') are Ferdinand's, and refer to the way Alexander the Great solved the problem of the Gordian knot.

Early modern Europe

You can see that, though there were differences, the 'new monarchs' had roughly the same ideas. Their people, too, were coming to feel that loyalty to the king was absolutely right, and that treason was one of the worst of crimes. It was certainly punished as though it were. Besides this feeling about the king, people were being held together by a feeling that they were fellow-members of a nation, not of a certain town or county. It was more important, for example, that you were an Englishman than that you had been born in Bristol or Warwickshire – though you would still be proud of that, too. So these monarchs were usually ruling not just states, but 'nation-states'.

States of this type were taking firm shape all over Europe,

in addition to the 'Big Three' which we have already been looking at. Furthest west, the PORTUGUESE, under the royal family of *Avis*, were the first European nation to explore the oceans and set up an empire overseas. In the north, the SWEDES rose against their Danish rulers during the 1520s, and rallied round their new royal family of *Vasa*. The Netherlands, or Low Countries, had an interesting development. They were ruled during the fifteenth century by the dukes of Burgundy (page 21), who used many of the usual methods – councils, educated secretaries, money, a splendid court and expensive soldiers – in an attempt to forge a strong state. But there lacked national unity among Netherlanders. That is, until late in the sixteenth century, when the northern Netherlanders rose against the Spanish descendants of the old dukes, and formed themselves into the DUTCH nation.

The States of Western and Eastern Europe in the 16th century

Spanish possessions, reign of Philip II
Other Habsburg lands
Political boundaries
Boundaries within the Empire

In eastern Europe there were special obstacles to the development of 'nation-states' and 'new monarchies' among the Slav peoples. The whole Balkan region was part of the huge empire of the Ottoman Turks. The Christian peoples who lived there had to obey the *pashas* (governors) appointed by the Sultan in Istanbul (the name the Turks gave to Constantinople, which they had captured in 1453). The Turks also broke up and partly occupied the kingdom of Hungary in 1526, and were a constant menace to their other neighbours. Despite this and other dangers, in Poland the nobles never agreed to become obedient to their king; two centuries later Poland was to pay for this weakness when the country was divided up between the kings of other states. Only in RUSSIA can we find, during this period, really successful kings. Here the Tartars and Mongols, who had held the south and east since the time of Jenghiz Khan, gradually weakened. As they did so, the *princes of Moscow* gained power. The two most famous were Ivan the Great (1462–1505) and Ivan the Terrible (1533–84). They claimed to be the heirs of the Byzantine emperors, and took the title of *Tsar* or *Czar* (Caesar) of all the Russias. But they had great difficulties which kept them busy in their own region, and were remote from the monarchs of the nation-states of western Europe.

The court of Suleiman I 'the Magnificent', who ruled the Ottoman Empire from 1520 to 1566. The picture is from a Turkish life of Suleiman written in 1579.

left: Ivan IV 'the Terrible'. The reconstruction was made in 1964 by the anthropologist M. M. Gerasimov, working from measurements of the Tsar's skull.

far left: St Basil's cathedral, Moscow. It was built between 1555 and 1560 by Ivan the Terrible with money from Kazan, the Tartar city he had captured in 1552. Its nine cupolas have been described as gay, extravagant, passionate; also as 'a nightmare in stone'. In Ivan's time the church was white – the colours were added in the seventeenth century.

Now let us see what this added up to. Quite close together, in western Europe, there was a fairly small number of states which were better organised and more firmly governed than anything in this area since the time of the Roman Empire. Ruling these states were kings, who were frequently ambitious and who naturally suspected the ambitions of other kings. They were always watching for chances to make themselves stronger, and on the look-out for dangers. This meant that they wanted to know what the other kings were up to.

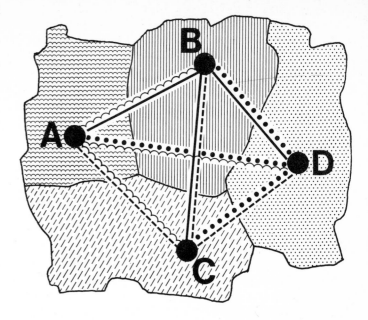

So they got into the habit of keeping agents at one another's courts.

Kings had always sent ambassadors to other courts when there was some special business to be done. When it was finished, the ambassadors returned home.

Now, although it was still possible to send a special ambassador for anything very important, kings began to agree to exchange permanent ambassadors, so that they could

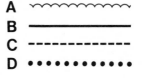

A	〰〰〰〰〰
B	————
C	- - - - - -
D	••••••••••

The antennae of princes Each ruler wishes to have his own means of communication with the capitals of other important rulers.

keep in touch with each other all the time. Naturally, kings who did this were on more or less friendly terms with each other; but even when the friendship was not very warm, even when there was a serious risk that the ambassador might be a spy or a plotter, kings found it useful to keep in contact like this. And, after all, the spying and plotting was a game that two could play.

Something like this had already happened on a small scale, among the little states which were crowded together in Italy. Now, after about 1500, the idea spread all over western Europe. International diplomacy, as we know it today, was beginning.

The diagram will give a rough idea of the way the courts of western Europe were linked by ambassadors in the sixteenth century. It is easy to understand that when all the main states were connected like this, every one was interested in anything that happened. What happened in country A might appear to be important only to the kings of B and of C; but the king of D, who seemed far away from it, might be very anxious that B or C should not become stronger. It meant that if trouble broke out anywhere in western Europe, all the kings were on the alert, either to keep the peace or, more often, to see what they could gain out of somebody else's difficulties.

You must have noticed on the maps on page 24 that two large and important countries of modern Europe did not become nation-states at this time. Italy and Germany, in fact, became even less united than they had been before. This was partly the price they paid for leading the rest of Europe in the Renaissance and the Reformation.

Italy
and the
Renaissance

The *Condottiere*, Bartolommeo
Colleoni; a life-size bronze
statue standing in Venice,
begun by the Florentine painter,
goldsmith and sculptor Andrea
del Verrochio in 1479. The
proud energy and determination
of the figure, the sureness and
delicacy of the workmanship
have made this statue seem, to
many people, a personification
of the spirit of Renaissance
Italy. When you have read more,
look at it again and see if you
agree.

left: The *Duomo* (cathedral), Florence. The *campanile* (bell-tower) was begun by the painter Giotto, 1266(?)–1337. The huge dome was built by the engineer and architect Brunelleschi, 1379–1446.

below left: La Rotunda, Vicenza, a villa designed in 1558 by Andrea Palladio, 1518–80. He inspired a style of architecture during the next two centuries which has been called Palladian.

below: The Annunciation, painted in 1486 by Carlo Crivelli, is almost as much an architectural as a religious picture. Artists were just beginning to understand the rules of perspective, giving a sense of depth and distance to a picture, and Crivelli showed off his skill here.

The word 'Renaissance' makes most people think of Italy, and rightly so. Many of the new Renaissance ideas came to life in Italy during the fifteenth century, and other nations got into the habit of looking to Italy as the home of culture and fashion. Renaissance ideas spread all over Europe in the fifteenth and sixteenth centuries, and it is hard to say when – or if – they died away.

The word 'Renaissance' also makes people think of art, and probably this is the easiest way to begin to understand what it was all about. You know about the styles of art which were used in the Middle Ages; remember, for instance, the Gothic cathedrals, with their towers and spires and pinnacles, their stained glass, their statues of saints elongated in flowing robes, their tombs of kings and knights with stiff effigies in brass and stone. Think of these, and then look at the pictures here. There is no need to try to decide which style you prefer. Perhaps you may think that they are both good, each in its own way. What is important is to see how different they are, for we are going to try to use these works of art to help us to understand the men who made them. What sort of men were they? What did they believe in? What was new about them?

Moses, carved about 1515 for the tomb of Pope Julius II by Michelangelo Buonarroti, 1475–1564.

below: Primavera (Spring) painted by Sandro Botticelli, 1445(?)–1510, for Lorenzo de Medici 'the Magnificent', the banker and poet who was also a statesman and ruler of Florence. The artist uses classical myth—the Three Graces, for example, and the goddess Flora—to try to capture the spirit of springtime.

The revival of classical learning

They may look different from the Middle Ages; but go back further. You must have noticed things about those Renaissance buildings and sculptures which remind you of the works of the Greeks and Romans. This likeness was deliberate. Renaissance men thought that civilisation had been at its highest during classical times, and they were trying to take their ideas from that ancient period. The word 'Renaissance' means Rebirth.

Scholars studied with fresh interest the ancient books which had been preserved in monastery libraries, copied by hand from still older copies. In the middle of the fifteenth century there came an invention which made it easy to produce many copies of these books: the printing press. The inventor was Johann Gutenberg, and for a time printing was known as 'the German art', but it spread quickly to many lands. Aldus Manutius of Venice became famous for printing Greek and Latin classics which were small and cheap enough for scholars to carry in their pockets, yet beautifully clear and easy to read.

In such books people studied the ancient poets, playwrights, historians and philosophers. They admired what the ancient writers said, and the way that they said it. A few Renaissance scholars even gave up their faith in Christianity, so as to believe exactly what the ancient philosophers had believed. Many, however, tried to make their religion fit in with the ideas of the great men of ancient times, especially Plato. We can see from the two paintings opposite, both by the same artist, that there was no difficulty in being a Christian and still admiring the pre-Christian teachers. This was not being disloyal to the Church, but it did mean that people were realising that the Church was not the only place where you could learn wisdom.

Renaissance scholars thought it important to speak and write correctly. A man speaks as he thinks, so an educated man should use words accurately and elegantly. During the Middle Ages Latin had remained the language spoken by educated men of all western European nations. Since it was alive, it was always changing; new words were coined, grammar became simpler and rougher. Now the learned men of the Renaissance wanted to use pure, correct Latin, the sort of language Cicero had used 1,500 years before. So they did. But this had one result which they had not expected. To keep Latin in what they considered to be perfect condition, they

The Virgin and Child (*right*) are part of an altar-piece painted between 1503 and 1508. Plato and Aristotle (*far right*) are the central figures in a large fresco, *The School of Athens*, painted between 1509 and 1512, in the Vatican. (Old Plato is thought to be a portrait of Leonardo da Vinci.) Both are the work of Raffaello Sanzio, 1483–1520, usually called Raphael.

Printing in Germany, 1568. This woodcut by Jost Amman was itself originally printed in the way it illustrates. The men in the background are setting type from cases. In front, the man on the left is positioning paper in a frame which will be fitted into the press, while the other inks the type with printer's balls – pads rolled first in ink and then over the type, which frequently led to uneven printing.

froze it. Only learned men were able to use it, it was so artificial. The Renaissance scholars turned the language they loved into a dead language.

Although it stopped being a living international language (we have still found nothing to replace it) Latin became the basic subject in boys' schools, with Greek in second place. In Tudor England many schools were either founded or refounded, and every town soon had its grammar school – Latin grammar, of course. Schoolmasters believed that the hard work, discipline and logic which a boy needed in learning grammar were good for his mind and character. They also believed that by carefully studying the books of the great classical writers boys would begin to understand how such great minds worked, and perhaps even begin to think in the same way. You must decide for yourself how much truth there is in this idea. Anyway, for at least three centuries Englishmen stuck to the Renaissance belief in a 'classical education', and there are still plenty of traces of this today.

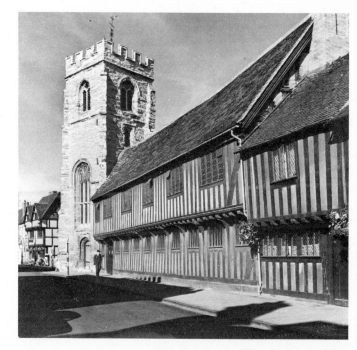

right: The old grammar school at Stratford-on-Avon where William Shakespeare was educated in the 1570s.

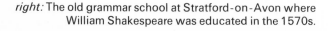

New 'classics' in 'new' languages

While Latin was gradually sinking into being only a scholar's language, the ordinary languages of Europe came into their own. Of course, people had always made poems and stories and songs in their everyday language; some of these had been great and famous, like Chaucer's *Canterbury Tales*, written before 1400, and Dante's *Divine Comedy*, written nearly a century earlier in Italian. Now that there were printed books, and people were more easily able to read for their own pleasure, writers were encouraged more to write for ordinary people.

There had been a feeling that it was not quite dignified for an educated man to write in the vernacular, in the common language. This notion faded. Some of the books which were written in the ordinary languages of different countries have turned out to be amongst the greatest books in European literature, and we now think of them as 'classics' just as much as the books written by ancient Greeks and Romans. Possibly the most famous of all was written in Spanish, about 1600: *The Adventures of Don Quixote*.

Don Quixote, the noble-minded but impractical knight, and Sancho Panza, his down-to-earth squire, have meant something to people at all times and in many lands. This is a still from a Russian film of 1957.

Julius Caesar

Romeo and Juliet

The Merchant of Venice

At the same time, Shakespeare was writing his plays in English. You will already know about them, but have you noticed how often Shakespeare uses ancient Roman stories? Or sets his plays in Italy? (Many of his plays, also, show a very strong feeling of pride in his own nation, the sort of feeling we discussed on page 24.) Shakespeare had been educated at the grammar school at Stratford-on-Avon. Even if it is true that he learned there 'small Latin and less Greek' he had the lively mind, the wide knowledge and the love of beauty which marked a true man of the Renaissance.

Discovery

From all this you will have seen that it was not simply a matter of *copying* the past. Renaissance artists and writers were *using* the ideas which they had found in the ancient world in order to make splendid new things. Inspiration is very different from dull imitation. St Peter's is not just a copy of the Pantheon; one is a fine Ancient Roman building, the other is a fine Renaissance Roman building. Men who were so eager in discovering the treasures of the past would surely be eager in discovering and understanding other things, too.

The Pantheon is a circular temple with a large window set in the apex of its dome. For many centuries afterwards builders lacked both the skill and the high-quality concrete to equal the engineering feats of the ancient Roman architects.

St Peter's, (*below*) the largest church in Christendom, is planned like a cross, with a high dome supported on huge pillars at the centre. Its building went on for most of the sixteenth century, and many artists in turn had a hand in the design, especially Bramante and Michelangelo.

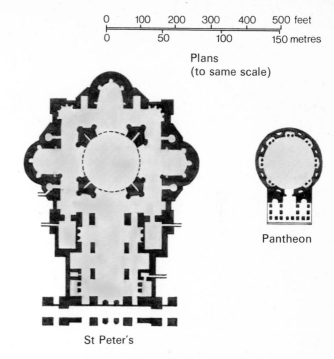

| 0 | 100 | 200 | 300 | 400 | 500 feet |
| 0 | | 50 | | 100 | 150 metres |

Plans
(to same scale)

Pantheon

St Peter's

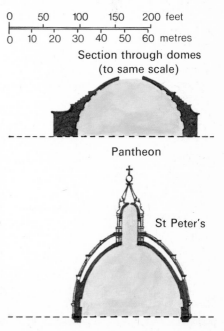

| 0 | | 50 | | 100 | | 150 | | 200 feet |
| 0 | 10 | 20 | 30 | 40 | 50 | 60 metres |

Section through domes
(to same scale)

Pantheon

St Peter's

The Ptolemaic Universe

The classical idea, best known in the version set down in the second century AD by the Alexandrian mathematician, astronomer and geographer Ptolemy, places the earth in the centre. It shows sun, moon and stars passing over and under a world which consists mainly of the Eurasian land mass. This theory was widely accepted during the Middle Ages.

The Copernican Universe

The system devised by Nicholas Copernicus, 1473–1543, and still accepted generally, shows the sun as the centre, with the earth spinning on its axis besides circling around the sun.

The pair of diagrams comes from *Harmonia Macrocosmica* by Andrea Cellari, published in 1660. They are not meant to be to scale.

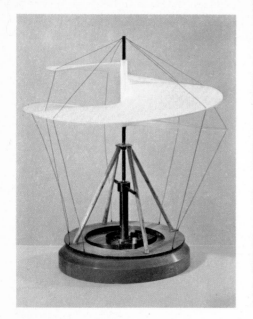

above left: A model built at the Science Museum, London, in 1952, from sketches by Leonardo da Vinci, 1452–1519. It represents a helicopter meant to carry one man and a power unit, and the idea of screwing through the air may have been inspired by children's whirligig toys. Leonardo also sketched 'ornithopters', birdlike machines with flapping wings.

above right: Many architects designed new towns on paper. This is the most complete survivor of the few which were actually built: Palma Nova, near Venice, 1593, planned by Vincenzo Scamozzi. The geometrical pattern is to provide good lines of fire for the garrison's guns, but we can hardly doubt that Scamozzi also thought it beautiful.

The Renaissance was the age of the great geographical discoveries, when sailors and soldiers from the nation-states of Europe penetrated seas and lands which no European had ever even dreamt of before. That is so immense a subject that we cannot discuss it here: it needs a book to itself. These discoveries may have had nothing to do with the study of Greek and Roman books, though Renaissance geographers knew Ptolemy's atlas, which was reprinted several times. Yet they happened at the same time, and must have helped to give men a feeling that there were all sorts of wonderful things to be discovered, if only people had the energy and intelligence to go and find them out.

Some tried to discover more about how the universe worked. In 1543 was published a book describing the theories of Nicholas Copernicus, a Polish priest, who claimed that the sun, not the earth, was the centre around which the universe revolved. Knowing what an outcry there would be, especially among some other churchmen, he delayed his book for many years, but gradually his ideas became known and believed.

There were many clever engineering and mechanical ideas. Leonardo da Vinci went so far as to devise flying machines, though they never flew outside the pages of his notebook. Many Italian engineers were less interested in the principles behind machines, more in hard, practical reality: artillery, for instance, and fortification. Yet they were not ignorant; military engineers were students of geometry.

Despite this progress, it took some time for the really great scientific discoveries to come. Since they were made after 1600, we need not discuss them now. It is worth remembering, though, that it was probably the Renaissance spirit of curiosity and enterprise which eventually led to the work of such men as Harvey, Galileo and Newton.

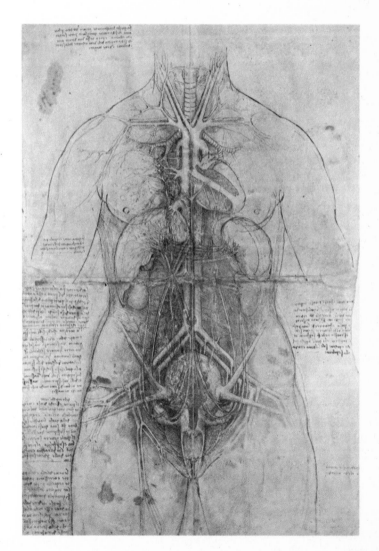

Pen-and-ink drawings of a lily (*left*) and human anatomy (*below*) by Leonardo da Vinci. Though it offended most people, Leonardo dissected over thirty corpses.

Men of the Italian Renaissance

We can recognise similar curiosity and technical skill if we look back to the artists of Renaissance Italy (pages 27–9). Notice that they had discovered how to use perspective, to give depth to their pictures. Notice, too, how lifelike they made their paintings and statues. All this shows more than skill. It shows that the artists intended to make their works as near the living thing as they possibly could. The pictures on this and the following pages tell us the same. The artists had a great interest in nature, in plants, in everything that breathed; but most of all they were interested in human beings.

Some statues and paintings show the human body, in action or at rest, in all sorts of attitudes. An artist, for instance, when making sketches for a painting of a battle, might draw the warriors nude, making sure that their bodies were in exactly the right positions, before attempting the final picture with clothes and armour. Such sketches also show how well an artist could portray human passion, like the fury of battle. We have already seen many examples of how portrait-painters tried to give a living likeness to their pictures.

Soldiers surprised while bathing — a subject which gives the artist an opportunity to show the human body in a great variety of poses. Contemporary engraving of Michelangelo's sketch for a fresco, *The Battle of Cascina*; the fresco was never painted, and the original sketch is lost.

Human beings, thought the men of the Renaissance, were God's finest work. Everyone should strive to make himself (or herself) as perfect as he could, should develop all the powers God had given him. The ideal man of the Renaissance was the complete, all-round man, and there were some who did indeed seem to live up to this, to be good at everything that was worth doing. You have already met Leonardo da Vinci as an engineer and an artist; he was outstanding in both roles. Leon Battista Alberti (1405–71) was even more astonishing. Here is a rough and shortened version of some of the things he says of himself in his autobiography:

'His genius was so many-sided that all the fine arts were his. Even the need to eat and sleep could scarcely keep him from his books. He excelled in warlike games. With his feet together, he could leap over the shoulders of men standing beside him. He had hardly an equal in throwing the javelin. An arrow shot by him could pierce the strongest iron breast-plate. He could throw an apple in the air higher than the highest roofs. He delighted in the organ and was considered one of the finest musicians. He turned to physics and mathematics. His mind was always busy. He was always agreeable and gay, though dignified. He could endure pain, cold and heat, showing that men can do anything with themselves if they will.'

He thought well of himself, but, it seems, he was not boasting without cause. From the writings of people who knew him we are certain that he had a great reputation. Below are some of the books he wrote and the buildings he designed. False modesty, thought the people of the Renaissance, was just as bad as empty boasting. A man should not overvalue himself, but he should not undervalue himself either.

A list of some of Alberti's works

Buildings

Fountain of Trevi, Rome
Palace of the Rucellai, Florence
Churches of St Sebastian and St Andrew, Mantua
Temple of the Malatestas, Rimini

Books

Philodexius, an imitation of an ancient Roman comedy which deceived experts.
On Building, the first architectural treatise printed. It describes classical design, proportion, method.
On Painting, which includes a discussion on perspective.
On Statuary, which considers the perfect proportions of the human body.

left: Baldassare Castiglione, 1478–1529, by an unidentified sixteenth-century artist.

right: Niccolo Machiavelli, 1469–1527, terracotta bust by an unidentified contemporary sculptor.

Naturally, they were very interested in how the best sort of men and women should behave. One of the most popular books of the sixteenth century, translated into many languages, was *The Courtier*. In this book Count Baldassare Castiglione reported a series of conversations which took place at the court of Urbino in March 1507. At least, he said that he was only reporting, but most people have thought that he added a great deal himself. You could already list, from the accomplishments which Henry VIII displayed and those which Alberti was so proud of, many of the qualities which were admired. Castiglione helps us to complete the picture:

A gentleman, he declares, should be good-tempered, easygoing but dignified. He should seem to do everything without having to try very hard; he should not play instruments, or games, so well that he must have spent far too much time practising such amusements, like a professional performer. His manners should not be a sort of glossy varnish, but should be naturally good. The courtier must be much more than a servant to his prince; he must advise and influence him towards wisdom and goodness.

This explains why Castiglione thought that being a courtier was one of the most important and honourable of jobs.

An even more famous book was written about the same time. This was *The Prince*, by Niccolo Machiavelli, and the sort of behaviour he recommended would have shocked Castiglione's courtiers. It has given a word to our language: Machiavellian. For Machiavelli taught that a ruler should think only of success. If he succeeded, everything he did was right. If he failed, he had been wrong. A prince, said Machiavelli, had to reckon on the weaknesses of other people, not their good qualities. It was more important to be feared than to be loved; though it was dangerous to be hated. A prince should keep his word, but only as long as this was useful to him. Above all, a prince should never allow himself to be deceived; in politics it was the cleverest deceiver who won.

Machiavelli's book was written in 1513 but not published until 1532. Ever since, he has been blamed for teaching rulers to be wicked. Did he? Was such a thing possible? There has been much argument about what he really meant. His defenders say that he was only describing what he saw going on all over Italy and Europe, that he was exposing the facts of political life for all to see. You already know something of the monarchs of Europe and will soon know more, so decide for yourself whether it is fair to blame Machiavelli.

Diplomats and mercenaries

Italy was divided into many states, but there were five big ones. The five were ruled in five different ways – a king, a Pope, two types of republic, and a duke. But mainly Italy was a land of city-states, in some ways like ancient Greece. Often a small city managed to remain independent; one, indeed, the republic of San Marino, has survived to the present day. Even when a city fell under the rule of a stronger neighbour, as Pisa fell to Florence, the people remained loyal to their own city; they were Pisans, not Florentines. Italian citizens were loyal, it is said, to their own bell-towers, their *campaniles*.

These cities were often rich. The men who ruled them, princes or merchants or nobles, were usually very intelligent and educated. They loved to be magnificent, and therefore employed architects, painters, writers. Also, penned together as they were in the narrow peninsula of Italy, they were constantly pushing against one another, each trying to make himself richer and stronger at the expense of others.

It is not surprising that, as we saw on page 26, the new pattern of diplomacy was begun among the states of Italy.

The most famous *campanile* of all, the leaning tower of Pisa. It was begun in 1174, during the period of Pisa's greatest wealth and power.

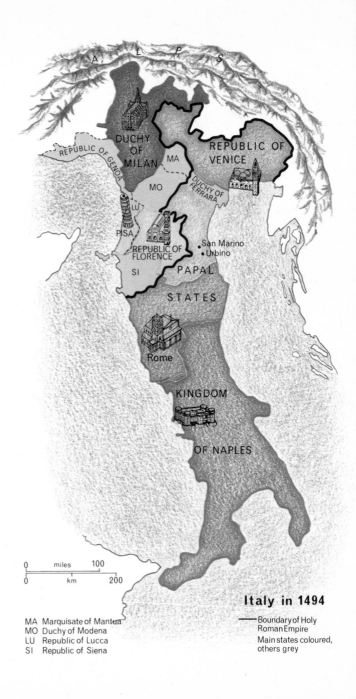

Italy in 1494

MA Marquisate of Mantua
MO Duchy of Modena
LU Republic of Lucca
SI Republic of Siena

—— Boundary of Holy Roman Empire
Main states coloured, others grey

40

This was especially because the merchants and bankers of Italy had been used to keeping agents in many cities, to help in their business deals, and it was only a short step from having trading and financial agents to having political agents. But diplomats could not always settle matters peacefully, and then soldiers were needed. The Italian states hired professional soldiers, men called *condottieri*, who contracted themselves and their followers to anyone who would pay them. Some of these mercenaries were foreigners, like Sir John Hawkwood who led the dreaded English 'White Company', but most were Italians. Sometimes they were lords of small cities themselves, like the Montefeltro family of Urbino, who needed the money to keep their city going. As time went on the *condottieri*, who were experts at their trade, conducted their wars more by manœuvres than by hard fighting. The statesmen and soldiers of beautiful, wealthy Renaissance Italy believed that cleverness and money could always win, and that they were the cleverest of all, far cleverer than the roughs from beyond the Alps. This was partly true, but only partly, as Italy was soon to learn.

Federigo da Montefeltro; born 1422, duke of Urbino 1444, died 1482. The portrait, painted about 1472 by Piero della Francesca, shows the duke, as usual, from the left; the right side of his face was badly damaged by the wound which also affected his nose.

The Montefeltro castle stands grimly on a great rock, with the little city of Urbino clustered about it. Within, though, it is a palace fit for patrons of art and learning. Among the clever details is the panelling of the duke's study.

The new pattern of war

The Italian Wars

In 1494 the French were invited to join in the disputes of the Italian states. Perhaps they would have come anyway, because their king had some sort of claim to the throne of Naples. The man who invited them was Ludovico Sforza, duke of Milan, who felt sure that he was clever enough to use the French to beat and terrify his enemies, especially the king of Naples, and then send them packing when he no longer needed them.

It worked. The powerful French army swept down Italy. All resistance crumbled. The king of Naples fled. The French had done what Ludovico wanted. Now it was time to get rid of them. The states of northern Italy, including Milan, turned against the French. Stuck in the south, the French felt trapped. They retreated hastily, and scrambled home as best they could. Ludovico had shown that Italian brains – especially his own – were more than a match for foreign brawn.

Unfortunately for Italy, he had not been quite clever enough. He had made the French really angry, and they were determined to have revenge. They had seen that Italy was rich, well worth looting or conquering. They had also learnt that Italian armies were not strong enough; though they had been forced out, when there had been any actual fighting the French had won. Furthermore, the king in 1494, Charles VIII, had been an exceptionally foolish young man; there was probably something seriously wrong with him, and he died within a year or two. The next king, Louis XII, was the former duke of Orleans, who had inherited a claim on Milan itself from his Italian grandmother. So in 1499 there was another invasion, and this time the story was different. Milan fell, and Ludovico ended his days in a French prison.

This was only the beginning. The French were not the only ones to have learnt that Italy was rich and divided, which meant weak. Spain was interested. Ferdinand of Aragon was king of Sicily as well as Spain, and he also had a claim to Naples. Besides, he had been invited to help in driving out the French in 1494–5, and had accepted.

Then there was the Holy Roman Emperor, Maximilian,

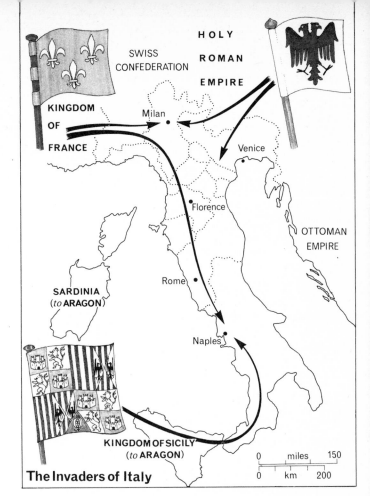

The Invaders of Italy

whose lands lay just across the Alps, in Austria and Germany. He claimed to be overlord of Milan and the rest of northern Italy. Two of his children had married two of Ferdinand's, and he agreed with the king of Spain that it would be a mistake to allow the French to have everything their own way in Italy. If there were going to be conquests and loot, he would have his share.

So they all piled in, and a long series of wars began. Usually the Spaniards and Imperialists fought against the French, with the Italian states shifting about, each trying to outwit everybody else. Some Italian statesmen – Machiavelli was one of them – foresaw how it must end: unless the Italians all joined together, they would all lose, and the winner would be one of the big powers from outside.

The Habsburgs and the kings of France

By 1519 there were no longer three big powers interested in Italy, only two. This map shows what had happened. As a result of marriages between the family of the Emperor Maximilian (their family name was Habsburg) and the Spanish royal family, and then some unexpected deaths, all the lands of both had been inherited by young Charles Habsburg. He was King Charles I in Spain, and was elected Emperor Charles V in Germany.

From the map you might think that he had enormous power, and so he had. But remember that he also had enormous problems. He had to rule over so many different peoples, each with its own language and laws and customs, each jealously anxious to prevent any of its money being spent on any other part of Charles' wide dominions. Yet Charles had to defend each and all of them against their enemies. Naturally, this young man felt that he dared not give way anywhere, that he must firmly hold his own. For if once this ramshackle empire began to crack, it might fall apart completely. Does he look likely to be equal to his gigantic task?

By this time, Francis I was king of France. He, too, was a young man, though older than Charles. He had a very high opinion of himself, and this had become higher than ever after the battle of Marignano. It happened in 1515, just after he had become king, and his army had won a great victory over the Swiss, those formidable pikemen whom nobody else had been able to stop.

Francis and Charles looked on each other as rivals, naturally. Besides, any king of France was bound to feel rather uneasy when he looked at the map, and saw Habsburg lands all round his own kingdom. Equally, the Habsburgs were bound to fear that France would act as a barrier, keeping their lands apart.

So it is not difficult to understand how the Italian Wars, which had lasted, off and on, since 1494, merged into the huge

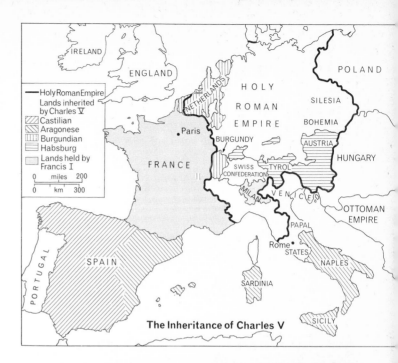

The Inheritance of Charles V

right: Charles V; born 1500, lord of Burgundy etc, 1506, king of the Spains etc, 1516, lord of Austria etc, 1519, Holy Roman Emperor 1519. Portrait by Bernhard Strigel, portrait painter to the Habsburgs, about 1517.

far right: Francis I; born 1494, king of France 1515. Portrait by Jean Clouet, about 1530.

duel between the two great powers of western Europe. You saw on page 14 how Henry VIII of England had tried to become the third great power, but he lacked both the strength and the skill to have much effect. This great duel, which began about 1520, lasted until about 1750. For over two centuries, whenever there was trouble in Europe, the king of France would take one side and the Habsburgs would take the other. Every European statesman could rely on it, and make his plans accordingly.

Since the struggle lasted so long, it is obvious that neither side really overcame the other decisively. But there were successes and failures, sometimes big ones. On the whole, Charles V did better than Francis I. This picture shows the famous battle of Pavia, 1525, when the Imperial and Spanish troops took Francis prisoner. Charles ended up with Milan as well as Naples, while the other Italian states understood that it was unwise to be his enemy openly.

Yet Charles died a tired and disappointed man. He learned that, as fast as he overcame one danger, another rose up behind him. If it was not Francis (who died in 1547), it was the Turks, or the Barbary pirates, or the Lutheran princes in Germany. So, admitting that he could not go on carrying such a burden, he divided his empire in two. (As you may be thinking, it was not the first time that a great empire had been split up, for one reason or another.) Then in 1556 he retired, to pass his last two years peacefully in a Spanish monastery. From this time onwards there were two branches of the Habsburg family, the Spanish and the Austrian.

Pavia, morning of 24 February, 1525. The French army had been besieging the city since October; its main camp lay near the country house of Mirabello (bottom left of picture). The Imperialist relieving force made a daring night march to break into the French position. After a fierce struggle the French were routed. This picture, probably painted in the Netherlands several years afterwards, represents the moment when Francis I is being taken prisoner and his army is fleeing. It is more a pictorial diagram than a work of art, but it clearly shows the types of soldiers and weapons involved.

Who gained?

If neither Francis nor Charles did very well out of their long wars, you may well ask who did.

Was it the soldiers? You may have noticed the various weapons being used at Pavia, especially the pikes and the guns. To use pikes properly, men had to stand close together in solid masses bristling with long, sharp spikes; but this made them a good target for guns, both the cannon and the hand-guns which were becoming more efficient. The casualties were terrible; wounds often meant a slow and painful death, for medical services were poor. The long sieges were probably even worse; in 1528, at Naples, hardship, hunger and plague wiped out most of the Spanish and German garrison, and the French besieging army as well. Soldiers endured all this danger and suffering in the hope of reward, loot and perhaps promotion. Pay was poor, and often late. Men were forced to rob nearby towns and villages to save themselves from starvation, though many a soldier did not need an excuse to rob civilians whenever he got the chance.

Soldiers boasted that theirs was an honourable life. They despised the humble peasants who stayed on their fields, enduring hard, grinding work and poverty instead of taking a chance in the army. But the only soldiers who were likely to do well out of the wars were a few high officers.

What about the civilians? If they lived in districts where fighting was taking place, they would have to feed and lodge soldiers. If they were very lucky, they would get some payment in return. If they were unlucky, they would be robbed or murdered. Anyone in a city which was stormed had no rights. In 1527 Rome was stormed by a half-mutinous Imperial army, and in the three days of terror which followed about 4,000 people were murdered, often cruelly.

Even people who lived all their lives in safety had to pay for the wars. Taxes were heavy. Despite this, most kings needed more money, and had to borrow from bankers; sometimes both kings and bankers went bankrupt.

Of course, there were rich people, and some of them may have become rich because of the wars. Even if they were not always paid in full, some merchants must have made big profits out of supplying the armies. When kings were so short of money that they had to sell lands, or pensions, or jobs, or titles, there were always people with the money to buy them,

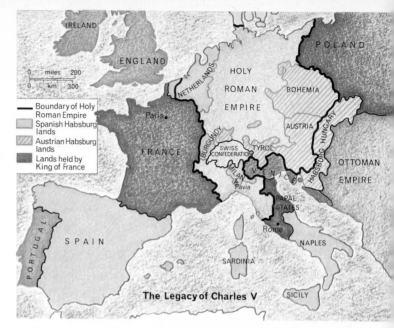

The Legacy of Charles V

and who must have thought that they were a good investment. Often these rich men were the king's own ministers and servants. What we cannot say for certain is how much these people gained from the wars, because many of them would probably have been able to enrich themselves anyway.

If any country could be expected to have profited from the wars of the sixteenth century, it would be Spain. Her armies won more often than the others, and Spain's power was so great that this has been called her 'Golden Century'. Yet many Spaniards have bitterly regretted that their country ever came under Habsburg rule, because, they argue, the Habsburgs made Spain spend men and money all over Europe, in wars which did not really concern her, and in the end there came overstrain and collapse.

Could any country even claim to have at least saved herself from invasion and conquest? You have seen that none of the great powers involved in the wars had started to fight as an act of self-defence.

As for Italy, she remained divided, with foreign dukes and viceroys in many of her richest states. For the next three centuries, wealthy tourists came to Italy to admire the Renaissance buildings and classical ruins, listen to the music, and buy pictures and statues to take home for their houses and gardens.

2. REFORMATION EUROPE

Germany and the Protestant Reformation

The Holy Roman Empire

If you remember how Charles the Great began the empire on Christmas Day in the year 800, you will know why it had been given this name. Now, 700 years later, did that name mean anything?

HOLY? The emperor was still supposed to be the chief protector of the Church, the partner of the Pope in leading Christendom. But nobody took this very seriously now, especially after all the furious quarrels between Pope and emperor during the Middle Ages.

ROMAN? As you see from the first map, it was really German. It is true that there were non-German peoples who were supposed to be part of the empire, but they lived round the edges, and usually took little notice of the rest of the empire.

EMPIRE? The emperor's government was very weak. It lacked the money and soldiers which it needed to keep order. Cities and nobles had to band together for their own protection, especially against those barons and knights who tried to make a living by robbery and blackmail. Some of the great nobles

Slavonic	Teutonic	Latin
Polish	High & middle German	French
Slovak	Low German	Italian
Slovenian	Dutch	Boundary of the Empire
Czech	Flemish	
Serbo-Croat		

The Holy Roman Empire c.1500
Language Divisions

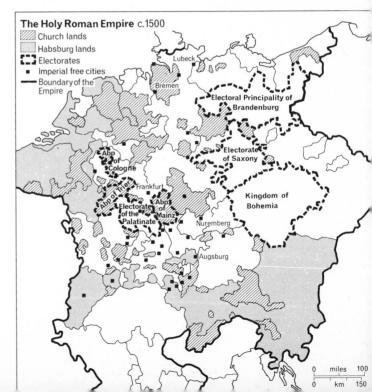

The Holy Roman Empire c.1500

Church lands
Habsburg lands
Electorates
Imperial free cities
Boundary of the Empire

had become so powerful that their lands were practically kingdoms. The greatest of these princes were the Electors, the seven who had the right to choose each new emperor. Naturally, these Electors were often unwilling to choose anybody who looked as if he might make them less powerful, make them and everyone else obey his government.

All the same, most Germans seem to have been proud of belonging to the German nation, loyal – though perhaps mainly in a sentimental sort of way – to the Holy Roman Empire, and they would be grateful for peace and good government. Emperor Maximilian I, whom you have already met and who reigned from 1493 to 1519, tried. He wanted to improve his councils and his law courts, like the other monarchs you have read about; to collect more money, and to raise an army of professional soldiers. (These men were called *landsknechts*, were rather like the Switzers, and many of them fought in the great wars.) Unfortunately, Maximilian never had enough money. He was so bad at paying his men that many of the *landsknechts* went to serve other kings, even the king of France, and instead of being the Imperial army they became just another set of mercenaries.

above: One of the most influential Electors of the time, Frederick III 'the Wise' of Saxony; born 1463, elector 1486, died 1525. This portrait was engraved by Albrecht Dürer in 1524.

Landsknechts on the march, about 1510–20. Woodcut by an unidentified artist. The men carry matchlock guns, their leaders halberds. The costumes and swords are characteristic of the landsknechts.

One reason why Maximilian never had enough money was that he was too fond of spending it: artists, tournaments, splendid armour and fine clothes, processions, hunting. One of the many works of art which he ordered was his *Triumphal Procession*, engraved by some of the finest German Renaissance artists. These few pictures from it, only 4 out of the 137 parts, will suggest how Maximilian enjoyed being a Renaissance prince, and suggest how much it cost him.

But even if he had been more careful with his money, Maximilian might never have been able to build up a strong government, because the Electors had no intention of letting

left: Maximilian I; born 1459, married Mary of Burgundy 1477, Emperor 1493, died 1519. Portrait by Dürer, 1519.

right: Maximilian was especially fond of Tyrol, and this picture is from a book on Tyrolean fishing, made for him about 1504. Fish are netted, cooked in a cauldron, and served picnic-style to the guests, while musicians play. Beyond, in the forest, stags are being hunted — one has taken to the water, and hounds are swimming after it. In the distance, daring huntsmen pursue chamois among mountain peaks.

him become their master, and they were powerful enough to stop him. The Electors did want Germany to be well ruled by a strong government, but it had to be a government which they would control. When they suggested plans for this, Maximilian would not have it. And, though the Electors were strong enough to stop Maximilian from getting what he wanted, he was strong enough to stop them from getting what they wanted. So Germany remained a collection of principalities and cities, only loosely held together.

Then there came a great religious conflict, which divided the nation more than ever before.

below: The ancient Roman idea of triumphal processions was adapted by Renaissance artists in paintings and engravings intended to symbolise their prince's power and splendour. Maximilian himself in 1512 dictated instructions for a series of 137 woodcuts displaying his grandeur. Many famous artists contributed, the main one being Hans Burgkmair. The pieces shown here are (*from left to right*):

1 One of the groups of horsemen carrying the standards of Maximilian's lands — here Alsace, Habsburg, Tyrol. 'In any land in which the Emperor has waged war, the man bearing the banner shall wear armour.' (Maximilian's instructions.)
2 Men dressed for jousting in the German style. (Maximilian was a great patron of tournaments of all sorts.)
3 Men dressed and armed for foot combat in the Hungarian style.
4 One of several cars carrying musicians and drawn by a variety of animals — this had a dromedary.

The Lutheran revolt

As you may have guessed, there was plenty of money about in Germany, at least in the hands of some people. Many of the nobles, and the merchants of the great cities, lived in luxury and gave plenty of work to the painters, carvers and metalworkers. In Augsburg were the headquarters of the two biggest banks in Europe, those of the Fugger and Welser families, who were just as important as Italian bankers like the Medici had been. Without their loans, many of the kings, nobles and bishops of Europe simply could not have gone on.

One such was Archbishop Albert of Mainz. He had been appointed in 1514, and had to borrow large sums from the Fuggers, partly to pay fees to the Pope. The Pope himself needed money, especially to pay for the rebuilding of St Peter's (page 33). So the Pope arranged with the archbishop that he should sell Indulgences in Germany, and that the money would be used to pay the archbishop's debt, and the remainder sent direct to the Pope. A Dominican friar named Tetzel was made salesman, and he travelled from town to town, gathering large crowds and urging them to buy Indulgences.

Jacob Fugger and his chief accountant, Matthäus Schwarz, painted in 1519. The shelves behind are labelled with the names of cities where the Fuggers had business — Lisbon, Rome, Milan, Venice, Cracow and Budapest, for instance, as well as German cities.

The regular rows of roofs belong to the Fuggerei, a quarter of Augsburg founded by Jacob Fugger in 1519. The houses, small but good, were occupied by poor people who paid a rent of only one Rhenish guilder a year. The Fuggerei has been called the first 'social settlement' in Europe.

What were these Indulgences? Even experts find it difficult to explain exactly. The general idea is something like this. If you do a good deed, this reduces the amount of punishment which you deserve for your bad deeds, and which God would make you suffer after your death before letting you into Heaven. Giving money to the Church is a good deed. If you wish, you can transfer this Indulgence which you have bought to a relative or friend who has died already, and who is now undergoing punishment. Thus you can let him into Heaven without suffering so much.

That is an extremely crude and simple explanation of the main idea behind a very complicated set of teachings; an expert would add a lot of 'ifs' and 'buts'. However, Tetzel was trying to sell Indulgences to simple people, and his explanation seems to have been very simple, too; perhaps even simpler. It seems that many of the people who listened to him thought that they could buy a ticket straight to Heaven for themselves and their friends.

In Saxony the Elector had, only a few years before, founded a new university. One of the professors of theology was an Augustinian friar named Martin Luther. For many years this man had been thinking very hard about what God most wanted a Christian to do before he deserved to go to Heaven. Luther had finally decided that God would be merciful to anyone who honestly believed and tried to do his best. Obviously, any true Christian would pray, would go to Church, would be kind to other people, would perform *good works*. But he would do these things because he believed, because he had *faith*. So faith in God was the important thing. It was what a Christian truly felt inside that counted, not the deeds which all could see.

You can imagine what Professor Luther thought of the way Tetzel was selling Indulgences.

above right: German printers sold verses and caricatures like this one of Tetzel. The two last lines of the first verse sum up what he was alleged to be preaching:
As soon as the guilder in the basin clinks
At once the soul into Heaven springs.

right: Martin Luther, 1483–1546. One of the many portraits by his friend Lucas Cranach the elder, 1472–1553, court painter to Elector Frederick the Wise from 1504.

All through the Middle Ages scholars in the universities had argued over various points of religion, and there did not seem to be anything very terrible in Luther's ideas. Luther thought that Tetzel was very wrong, so he did what was quite normal in such a case. He issued a challenge to debate Indulgences with anybody who believed as Tetzel did. He issued the challenge by writing out Ninety-five Theses (or arguments) against Indulgences as Tetzel had explained them, and pinning them to the church door in Wittenberg on All Saints' Eve, 1517.

The effect was far more than Luther or anybody else expected. The Ninety-five Theses were copied, taken to printers, sent all over Germany. For years people had been becoming more and more irritated with the Church, with its unceasing demands for money and its claims for privileges, for respect and obedience. It was not, men said, as if the churchmen were so good that they deserved all this; they just seemed to be making a soft living by telling other people how they ought to behave. Anyway, there was far too much money going to Italy, to be spent on all sorts of luxuries, when it ought to stay in Germany. This was the way thousands of Germans seem to have been feeling. Whether he intended it or not, Luther's challenge to Tetzel made him the champion of all those people who had been growing exasperated and angry at the way churchmen behaved.

There had been plenty of criticisms already of the clergy. You read on page 12 of Erasmus, the most famous Renaissance scholar in the northern part of Europe. His book *The Praise of Folly* had set all educated men laughing at the stupid things that happened in the Church. Erasmus did not mean to attack the teachings of the Church, only the faults of churchmen; but this sort of mocking meant that people had very little respect left for a Church which could not stamp out such faults. It was said: 'Erasmus laid the egg, and Luther hatched it.'

That remark, of course, was not very fair to either Erasmus or Luther. They had not caused the discontent, and many other people had said and written sharp words about the Church. Besides, people in Germany were feeling discontented, worried, restless because of many other things than religion.

Germany was not the only country where people were discontented. It seems that all over Europe the population

had increased, so that there were more people than ever before, all needing work, food and shelter and clothing. But there was not enough to go round, and therefore prices rose; a loaf of bread, for example, could cost four times as much in 1600 as in 1500. People's incomes did not rise as quickly as the prices; this was as true of the landlord's rents as it was of the workman's wages. Historians argue about exactly how and why all this came about, but they agree that it must have been behind much of the poverty and suffering, crime and rebellion which disturbed many countries in the sixteenth century. In Germany there was no strong national government to keep order.

The peasants were angry because landlords were trying to revive and enforce feudal rights which had been given up years before.

The landlords were worried because their money seemed to buy less and less each year, which was why they tried to get more out of the peasants.

The knights feared that the princes were becoming too strong, and some of them were desperate that they might lose their freedom.

The merchants were tired of having to pay tolls and protection money, and to guard against robbers, as their goods travelled from one part of Germany to another.

The princes, with the Electors in the lead, were determined to build their lands into strong little states.

With so much annoyance and anxiety and ambition disturbing people, it is easy to understand that it might not take a great deal to cause serious trouble to burst out.

Luther became famous at once. The leaders of the Church decided that he must be made to withdraw his Ninety-five Theses. He refused. Learned men were sent to argue with him, who were able to show that what Luther had said meant that he disagreed with many of the most important teachings of the Church. They thought that this would be enough to show Luther that he had been mistaken, and that he would draw back. But the opposite happened. Luther was an obstinate man, and a brave one. He now went on to attack many other beliefs of the Church. It was lucky for him that the Elector of Saxony, though he did not agree with much of what Luther said, refused to let any harm come to his famous professor.

Now Luther learned the value of the printing press. He poured out his ideas, in pamphlet after pamphlet. He said that priests were not nearly as important as they thought they were, and that people could get to Heaven without their help. He said that Christians should read the Bible for themselves, and that this would be a better guide to what they should believe than anything the Church could tell them. He said that the Church was far too proud and rich, and that it was the duty of the nobles and princes to put this right – which gave them a good excuse to confiscate the wealth of the Church, if they wanted to.

The Dance of Death has a message: we are all only mortal, no matter how great or humble we may be, rich or poor, old or young, and death can come at any moment. It was a common theme in the fifteenth and sixteenth centuries, and in 1538 Holbein used it in a series of forty-nine engravings which cover all the classes of German society. In these four examples Death is summoning (*left to right*) the duke, the child of a poor family, the husbandman, and the new-married lady.

All over Germany, people were confused. From the princes down to the peasants, some were for Luther, some against. The new young emperor, Charles V, came to hold a Council of the princes of the empire, or Diet, as it was called. It was held in the old Rhineland city of Worms, and Luther was summoned to appear before it. He was given a safe-conduct, but still it was dangerous; such a safe-conduct had been broken before. He went to Worms, stood before the emperor and the princes, said what he believed, and was told to change his ideas. Luther, brave as he was, hesitated, overawed. He went away to think. Could he possibly be wrong? Next morning he came before the Diet again. He had recovered his determination:

'Here I stand. I can do no other. God help me. Amen.'

Scholars have doubted if he ever actually spoke those famous words, but they certainly express his attitude. There was to be no withdrawal. The Diet declared him an outlaw, but it kept its promise of safe-conduct. He could go home in peace. After that he would have to be prepared for arrest, possibly death.

On his way home from Worms, Luther disappeared. He had been carried off by armed men, locked in a castle. But

above: Luther before the Diet of Worms, 18 April 1521; the scene as reconstructed for a film in 1953.

Since the 1460s discontent among the peasants in western and south-western Germany had frequently exploded into violence. They often tied a *Bundschuh*, or peasant's boot, to a pole and used this as their standard of revolt. Here armed peasants, carrying a *Bundschuh* flag, stop a knight; woodcut from a book published in Augsburg, 1532.

these men turned out to be friends, servants of the Elector of Saxony, who wanted still to protect Luther, but without doing it openly now that Luther was under the ban of the empire. In the castle of the Wartburg, in the study which was provided for him, Luther wrote and wrote. He began a German translation of the Bible; it was not the first, but Luther had the gift of being able to write in a lively, vivid and homely way that people could easily understand and remember. He wrote hymns with strong, stirring words; you may know 'A safe stronghold is our God'. His ideas spread.

More and more people came to believe as Luther did. They became Lutherans. If those people happened to be princes, or powerful nobles, or rich merchants who controlled cities, then they often made their followers or fellow-citizens become Lutheran, too.

Luther had started a religious revolution, and it was more than he could control. All sorts of discontented people tried to use his name. In 1522 some of the Rhineland knights tried to overthrow the archbishop of Trier, claiming to be Lutherans – as, indeed, some of them were – and had to be put down by the soldiers of some of the princes. Worse still, many of the poor people and the peasants thought that Luther was preaching a revolution which would not stop at merely praying. They got the idea that it was God's will that the lords and rich men should treat the poor as brothers, should stop holding them down, should give them a large share of their wealth. A great revolt, the Peasants' War, broke out in 1524, and spread through south-western and central Germany during that and the next year. It was encouraged by preachers who claimed to be Lutherans. Luther was horrified. He knew that princes, lords and rich men were often hard and cruel, but thought that Christians should put up with this, and concentrate on serving God instead of causing trouble, disorder, destruction and death. He thought that anyone who twisted his, Luther's, teachings into an excuse for rebellion was leading people to put the wrong things first, and must be very wicked. So Luther wrote another pamphlet, *Against the Murdering, Thieving Hordes of the Peasants*. He urged the princes to crush the peasants mercilessly. The princes did not need urging. At first the peasants won victories, but they were no match for the trained *landsknechts* whom the princes soon hired to fight for them. In their thousands, the peasants were slain in battle or executed afterwards.

Two of the leaders of the Peasants' War; engraved twenty years later by Hans Sebald Beham.

The princes decide

Now, with knights and peasants beaten, the princes were the people who could decide what would happen to Germany, in religion as in most things. Several principalities and cities became Lutheran. Just as many remained Catholic. These, combining with the emperor, tried to make the others return to the Catholic Church. The Lutheran rulers protested; that is how they came to be known as 'Protestants', a name which eventually spread to all the people who broke away from the Catholic Church. Fighting broke out in Germany between the Catholic and Protestant rulers. It was the first of the Religious Wars of the sixteenth century.

As you know, the Emperor Charles V had many tasks which took up his time and strength. Besides, he would have preferred to settle the trouble by persuasion instead of force, if he could. So it was not until 1546, the year when Luther himself died, that he came with an army to Germany. In 1547 he gained complete victory over the Protestant princes at the battle of Mühlberg. But even now the Lutherans would not agree to his attempts to win them over by offering some small changes in the Catholic Church (and the Pope might not have agreed, anyway). So, in spite of his victory, Charles had failed. Then some of his own supporters, fearing that he was becoming too powerful, treacherously attacked him. The emperor, defeated and disgusted, fled from Germany.

It was stalemate, and both sides had to admit it. In 1555 the Religious Peace of Augsburg was signed. This said that each prince had the right to decide the official religion in his lands for all his people. Whoever ruled the state also controlled its religion.

The Lutheran Reformation in Germany had ended by giving each prince more power, though this meant that there was now less chance than ever of the emperor being able to set up a strong government over the whole land. Meanwhile, other kings outside Germany had 'Reformed' their churches. You have seen how Henry VIII of England, though he always claimed to be against Lutheranism, had given himself the same sort of power over the Church in his kingdom. The kings of Denmark (who then ruled Norway, too) and Sweden became Lutherans. Each king had his own reasons, and it is very difficult to say how much each of them was genuinely religious, or was greedy for the wealth of the Church, or needed the extra power. Perhaps they themselves would not have been able to sort out their true motives. The result, anyway, was that the Lutheran Reformation did not create one new Church, but many; and each one was organised by the government of its state.

Luther had not planned to found all these churches. He had not even planned to break up the Catholic Church, which had been the only Church in western Europe for a thousand years. None of these enormous deeds can have been in anybody's mind that autumn day in Wittenberg when he put up his Ninety-five Theses. All the way through his career since then, Luther had been arguing and fighting his way forward,

below: Charles V at Mühlberg; painted in 1548 to celebrate the victory, by Tiziano Vecelli, 1490(?)–1576, usually called Titian.

gradually working out his ideas. Because of this, it is easy to find him saying different things at different times. He never sat down to bring all his ideas together in a neat, logical system, in one book where his followers could find all the answers.

The next great leader of the Reformation was to do this.

left: Gustavus Vasa (Gustaf Wasa); born 1496, led Swedish revolt against Denmark 1521, king 1523, took control of Church 1527, died 1560. Part of a full-length portrait by an unidentified painter, about 1542.

below left: Maurice of Saxony, 1521–53. Though a Lutheran, he helped Charles V against the Lutherans in return for the title of Elector. Then he suddenly turned against Charles in 1552. Portrait by Cranach.

57

The Puritan Churches

Title page of the first edition.

Title page of the first
English edition.

Calvin and his creed

John Calvin was born in north-east France in 1509. He went to the University of Paris, where he became a brilliant scholar. Like a true son of the Renaissance, he was especially good on the classics. He met other students, German Lutherans, and liked their ideas. But his keen and exact mind was not completely satisfied, and he began to think things out very carefully.

The university authorities discovered that Calvin no longer believed in the Catholic Church, and he had to flee from Paris and from France. He came to the Swiss city of Geneva, where there was a great deal of religious argument going on. (At about the time when Luther began the Reformation in Germany, another religious leader had been doing much the same in Switzerland. His name was Zwingli, and his teachings had led to fighting between the different cities and cantons of the Swiss Confederation. Zwingli had been killed in a battle, but trouble continued.)

Calvin was asked to stay and help the Protestant preachers in Geneva. He agreed, and began to teach his own ideas. These were very stern and very thorough, so that many people objected. After a couple of years, he was told to leave. He was a peaceful man, and went gladly.

What were these ideas of Calvin? He set them out in 1535 in a book called *The Institutes of the Christian Religion*. In later years he enlarged the book, but only to explain what he meant in more detail; he never changed his main ideas. This turned out to be a tremendously important book, a book which was to guide the lives of millions of people and to change the history of many lands, and it was the work of a young scholar of twenty-six. Though it is impossible to explain the book in a few words, it is possible to give a simple version of some of Calvin's main beliefs; for, like most of the creeds which have moved millions of ordinary people, the main things can be understood simply.

The basic idea was that people – *all* people – were naturally wicked. Adam and Eve had passed on their Original Sin to the entire human race. Because we are all evil, we all deserve to go to Hell; in justice, God should send us all there.

But God is not only just. He is also merciful. So, out of sheer kindness, He has chosen, or *elected*, some people to be saved. It is not that these people can possibly have done anything to deserve to go to Heaven, only that God is so good. Nobody can earn his way into Heaven.

THE ELECT

Mankind wicked and worthy of damnation

left: John Calvin: born 1509, first came to Geneva 1536, returned 1541, died 1564. Painter unidentified.

right: Calvinist minister preaching in St Peter's Cathedral, Geneva, shown in a sixteenth-century woodcut.

God is all-knowing and all-powerful, so He knew long ago which people were going to be saved, and which damned. So each one of us has been *pre-destined*, and there is nothing that we can do about it . . . That is what Calvin believed.

You may remember that Muhammad, 900 years before in Arabia, had also taught that God, Allah, had decided everything in advance. And you may remember that, instead of thinking that this meant that they could all sit down and let God get on with the job, Muhammad's followers had taken up their spears and rushed out to do God's work. Calvin's followers were rather similar. Though they did not go out to conquer empires, they did believe that they must try to live as nearly as possible according to what God liked.

Some of them, including Calvin himself, felt that God had called upon them to serve Him, to be the tools by which God would carry out His purpose. Nobody could be sure that God had chosen him to be one of the Elect, but it did seem reasonable to think that anybody who refused to lead a good life was not. For those who chose to lead godly lives, there could be no half-heartedness. They must always be on their guard against every sort of sin, they must sustain each other within their Church, and they must cast out the unworthy, the sinners who might corrupt the rest.

Geneva, the Puritan city

In 1541 Calvin was invited back to Geneva. By now, the most important citizens had come to think that they needed somebody of his firmness; it would strengthen the city altogether, they thought. But there were many who thought otherwise. Calvin himself feared the strain, the arguments and struggles, but he thought that God wished him to go back to Geneva. So he accepted. There were struggles, it is true, but he eventually gained unchallenged authority in the city – his enemies called him 'the Pope of Geneva' – and held it until his death in 1564.

Though he was so powerful, Calvin was never prince, or bishop, or mayor. He did not seek such offices. In his Church there were no such things as bishops, only plain 'ministers'. Any man who felt that God wished him to be a minister must first have a good education. Then he would be strictly examined by those men who were already ministers. If he passed, he would be presented to the city council. If they thought he was suitable he would be allowed to preach to the people. If they approved, he could at last be admitted as a minister, and he could be invited to look after a congregation. If he did not perform his duties well enough, he would be dismissed and become an ordinary citizen once more.

One of the main duties of a minister was to preach. Calvin, like some of the other Reformers, thought that ornaments and ceremonies harmed people, by taking their minds off serious things. This was true generally, they thought, but most of all in church. So the inside of a church ought to be very plain, and the services ought to be very simple. Calvin did allow music, for the singing of hymns and psalms, but the most important part of the service was the sermon, when the congregation would be made to think very seriously about their religion.

Anyone who led a bad life, or who did not attend church and listen to sermons often enough, would be made to repent and do penance in public, before the whole congregation. If this did not make him mend his ways, he could be expelled from the congregation. That may not seem a very heavy punishment, but, since all Geneva was Calvinist, it also meant poverty and exile.

This stern discipline was enforced by the minister, and also by the 'elders'. These were the leading men in each congregation, and usually seem to have been at least as powerful as the minister, often more so. Between them, they saw that no sin in their congregation remained undetected and unpunished. To cover the whole of Geneva there was a church council called a consistory. The members were six ministers and twelve elders. If it discovered anything which it thought too big for it to deal with, the consistory could ask the city council to take action; the city council could be relied upon to do so.

See how different this was from the Catholic Church, where authority belonged to the Pope and the bishops, and from the Lutheran churches, controlled by kings and their bishops. In Calvin's Church all the members – ministers, elders, and congregation – kept each other to strict standards, and did not take their orders from above. The city council and the Church consistory worked as partners; neither gave orders to the other. In fact, the Calvinist Church always got its own way. Calvinists from other countries, especially France, flocked to Geneva and were allowed to become citizens. Calvin's opponents either left the city or were punished, sometimes with torture and death.

Calvin had made a tough new Church which knew exactly what it believed, and which was organised to stand on its own feet.

The way of life which Calvin enforced in Geneva was very strict, or puritanical. That is a word which is often loosely used nowadays, but it began as a description of the behaviour of 'Puritans', and this was another name for people who thought more or less as Calvin did about religion. Geneva,

St Peter's Cathedral, Geneva, austerely stripped of medieval decoration, and with the pulpit rather than the altar dominating the congregation. This was where Calvin preached.

right: Puritans destroying church ornaments, from a book describing the troubles in the Netherlands, published in 1583.

far right: The central building of Calvin College, Geneva, erected in 1558.

before Calvin took charge, had been a city where any sort of conduct was permitted – rowdiness, drunkenness, immorality. It needed to be cleaned up. But it is going too far to whip a young woman for singing 'profane' words to a hymn tune, or to arrest the mother and the bridesmaids for dressing a bride too gaily.

Because of cases like that, because Puritans disapproved of many forms of amusement – feasting, dancing, acting – and because they dressed in plain, sober clothes, they came to have an unpleasant reputation. If you say 'Puritan' now, many people think of somebody like this; long-faced, sour, narrow-minded, and perhaps with a cruel delight in making other people feel miserable. But the picture is a caricature, not a true portrait. Let us now look at the other side of the Calvinist, Puritan character.

They worked hard, they were honest, they did not waste their money on, for example, fine clothes or drink. It is not surprising that many of them became rich. Some historians have argued that this had a great deal to do with the development of modern business methods, especially with the saving and investing of money which is called 'capitalism'. That has not been proved; you know that there had been several great money-men long before there were Calvinists, and some of the richest bankers and merchants of sixteenth-century Europe were Catholics. Besides, thrift and honesty alone are not usually enough to make men millionaires. It is true that many prosperous merchants during the next two centuries were Calvinists, but it would be very difficult to prove that there was a connection between their religion and their wealth.

Because they disliked laziness and begging, Puritans have been accused of being mean, hard on the poor. In Geneva, though, Calvin set up a special order of deacons whose duty was to look after the poor of each congregation.

Calvin, as might have been expected, set great value on education. He supported the college and academy in Geneva especially because he wanted good ministers to be trained there. It became one of the customs of Calvinists, however, to encourage everyone to get as good an education as possible. After all, it was a valuable training for the young to make them work hard at school and to discipline their minds, and an educated man would surely have a better understanding of the Scriptures than an uneducated one.

From Calvin's Geneva the new Reformed religion soon spread into several countries of Europe, and to the New World.

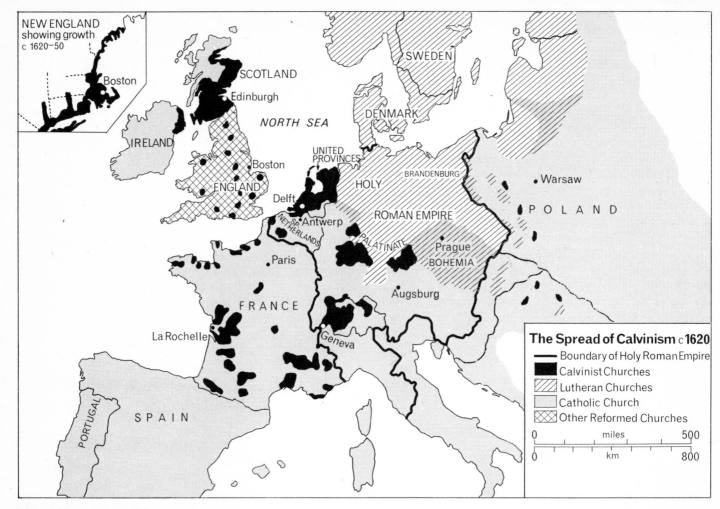

The Spread of Calvinism c **1620**

— Boundary of Holy Roman Empire
■ Calvinist Churches
▨ Lutheran Churches
▢ Catholic Church
▩ Other Reformed Churches

0 ———— miles ———— 500
0 ———— km ———— 800

NEW ENGLAND showing growth c 1620–50

Calvinism spreads

This map shows you how far, in about a century, Calvinism spread. Compare it with the map on page 57, which shows the Lutheran lands. Even the very short notes which follow will let you see what an important effect Calvinism had upon the history of several of the lands where it took root.

FRANCE. Dedicated ministers came from Geneva and gained many converts. Several nobles became Calvinists; some sincere, some because they hoped to use religious strife to gain more power. Savage religious wars broke out in 1562; the most

notorious incident was the Massacre of Huguenots (French Protestants) on St Bartholomew's Day, 1572. The wars ended in 1598, after Henry IV, who was the rightful king but a Calvinist, became a Catholic. Most Frenchmen were ready to accept this. Henry guaranteed freedom to the Huguenots, and gave them several fortified places, one of the most important being La Rochelle, to hold as safeguards.

NETHERLANDS. There was discontent, for many reasons, with the rule of King Philip II of Spain, who had inherited the Netherlands from his father, the Emperor Charles V.

below: St Bartholomew's Day in Paris, 24 August 1572. Admiral Gaspard de Coligny, leader of the Huguenots, had been shot earlier and was lying wounded in bed. As the picture shows, murderers broke in, stabbed him to death, then flung his body from the window. Many others, men, women and children alike, were butchered. This is part of a French print published shortly afterwards.

Rebellion was led by William of Orange, 1568. The southern Netherlands remained Catholic, held by Spain. The northern Netherlands, especially the maritime merchant province of Holland, became Calvinist. The north won its independence (in practice, 1609; officially, 1648), and became the United Provinces.

The Dutch became the foremost sailors and merchants of Europe during the seventeenth century, with an empire in the East Indies. This was also the great age of Dutch painting. You can argue about how much Puritanism was involved.

ENGLAND. The Church of England, as begun by Henry VIII and revived by Elizabeth I, was not Protestant enough to satisfy many Englishmen. There were increasing demands in Parliament for the Church to be made more Calvinist, especially for bishops to be abolished. Eventually this Puritanism was one of the causes of the English Civil War which began in 1642, as will be explained more fully in a later section of this book.

NEW ENGLAND. In 1620 a ship-load of Puritans who found it impossible to worship freely in England settled on the north-eastern coast of North America. Nowadays they are known as the 'Pilgrim Fathers', some of the most important founders of the U.S.A.

SCOTLAND. Opposition to Mary Queen of Scots (Catholic, brought up in France) was led by the Calvinist preacher John Knox. Mary fled in 1568, after a short civil war. The new king, James VI, still only a baby, came under the control of the Calvinists, or Presbyterians as they were called in Scotland. (A 'presbytery' was roughly the same as the Geneva 'consistory'.)

Presbyterianism got a firm hold in most of Scotland, and during the next century it showed vividly some of the best and the worst things about this sort of Puritanism. Schools flourished in every town and village. The 'dominie' or schoolmaster of even a remote village would normally be a man of learning, often with a university degree, and would be much respected by his neighbours. The Scots came to value education, and ordinary children in Scotland had a much better chance of being well educated than in the far richer kingdom of England.

Yet this education did not prevent these same people from being fanatical and cruel witch-hunters. They firmly believed that the Devil was always about, cunning and strong, ready to pounce. Men and women were thought to give themselves to the Devil, and to receive magical powers from him in return. These witches had to be discovered, questioned and tested and tortured until they confessed, and then killed. There is no way of telling exactly how many people, mostly women, suffered and died as witches during the seventeenth century in Scotland, but there must have been several thousands. It is reported that when one professional witch-finder was discovered to be a cheat and sentenced to be hanged, he confessed before his death to having had over 200 women, in England as well as Scotland, executed as witches; he had collected a fee of twenty shillings from the local authorities for every 'witch' he had 'discovered'.

Was there something about Calvinism which made Puritans especially prone to witch-hunting? Accusations of this sort have been made. Witch-hunting, however, was nothing new. There had been ugly outbreaks, for instance, in France and Germany during the fifteenth and sixteenth centuries. Often, we should also remember, the accused people believed themselves to be witches, learned professors of magic or priests of ancient gods. This kind of thing could happen in Catholic and Protestant countries, and in spite of Renaissance education. Undoubtedly in the seventeenth century Puritan lands were badly affected, not only Scotland but also England during the Civil War and New England as late as the 1690s. Before jumping to conclusions we should think of all the Calvinists who did not become witch-hunters, and all the people of

By the roadside at Forres, Elgin, stands this memorial to the cruelty with which witches were traditionally treated.

In the village of Durrisdeer in Dumfries-shire, is the oldest surviving school house in Scotland. It was built about 1695.

other religions who did. The argument is rather like the one about Calvinism and capitalism, mentioned on page 61.

You must have noticed, as we went from country to country, how often the Calvinists were involved in rebellion and civil war. This was not because Calvin had preached revolution; he had, in fact, preached patience and obedience whenever possible. Yet Calvinism was a fine religion for fighters. They knew exactly what they believed. They felt sure that they were doing what God wanted, and that in the end they were bound to win. They were used to strictness and discipline. They were used to working together inside their congregations, and, if there was the need for it, each congregation could fend for itself when other congregations had been destroyed by the enemy.

This map shows what happened to Europe during the Reformation of the sixteenth century. The main Protestant churches, Lutheran and Calvinist, took over most of northern Europe. Lutheranism came first, and usually became the state Church because the government, the prince, wanted it. Calvinism came rather later, when those countries which were going to become Protestant peacefully had already done so. Therefore the Calvinists had to fight for their religion, and often fought successfully.

The old idea of the Middle Ages, which had lasted a thousand years, that there was one Church for all the nations of western Europe, had been shattered. But the Reformed churches did not take over the whole of western Christendom. The old Church, as you see from the map, was unshaken in many countries, and overcame the Protestant challenge in others.

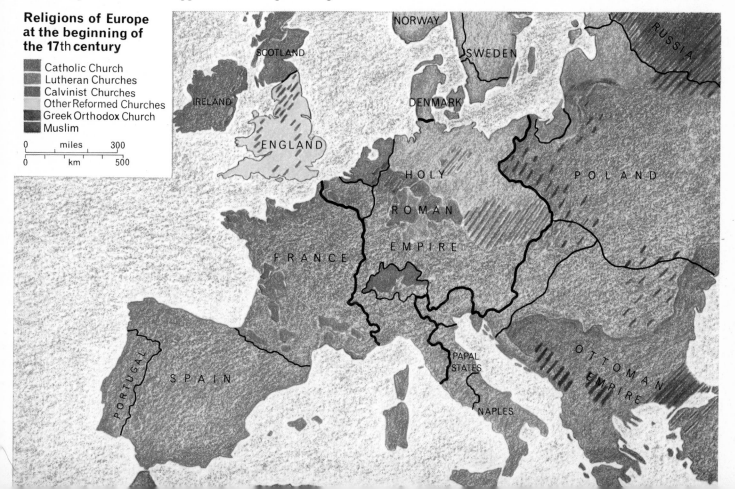

Religions of Europe at the beginning of the 17th century

- Catholic Church
- Lutheran Churches
- Calvinist Churches
- Other Reformed Churches
- Greek Orthodox Church
- Muslim

miles 300
km 500

The Catholic revival

The Spanish Inquisition

There had been many attempts to improve and reform the Catholic Church before Luther's outburst in 1517. If they had succeeded, probably Luther would never have done what he did, there might never have been a Reformation. Most of the attempts had failed, but there was one land where the Catholic Church had been reformed and strengthened several years before the Protestant Reformation. This was Spain.

Spain had had special religious problems. There had been many Muslims in Spain and the last Muslim kingdom had been conquered only in 1492. There had also been many Jews, for these people had been more kindly treated in Muslim lands than where Christians held power. Now most of these Muslims and Jews were obliged to join the Catholic Church, often under threat of death or exile. This sort of 'conversion' did not make them sincere Christians. Often it was more likely to make them hate Christianity, and carry on with their own religion in secret.

Everybody in Spain realised this. It was dangerous. Would these 'New Christians' betray the king if they got the chance? Especially if Spain were attacked by Muslims, like the Moors, or the Algerian pirates, or the mighty Turks? Worse still, there was the danger that they would not only go to Hell themselves, but that they might corrupt people who would otherwise have been good Christians and gone to Heaven. It was to guard against these dangers that Ferdinand and Isabella had founded the Spanish Inquisition (page 23). At the same time the Church in Spain had been made very much more strict and efficient. With the example and the leadership especially of Cardinal Ximenes de Cisneros, the bishops tightened the rules and weeded out slackness and laziness. By the time the Protestant Reformation began, the Spaniards were fiercely proud of their Church, as they were loyal to their king, and the tiny handful of Spaniards who tried to become Protestants were soon wiped out by the Inquisition.

Most people have heard of the Spanish Inquisition, and think of it as having been terribly cruel. It is easy to understand how it got that reputation, especially in Protestant countries. For one thing, everything was secret up to the sentencing of the convicts, and this was a spectacular affair, with processions, the prisoners wearing special gowns called *sanbenitos*, their sentences being read out, and many being led off to punishment. Some were burnt at the stake, others sent to prison or to row in the galleys, or flogged, or fined.

What had gone on before this *auto-de-fé*, as such ceremony was called? How had the victims been caught, and how had they been persuaded to confess? Like any secret police, the Inquisition used spies and informers, carried out its arrests quietly by night, tried to break down its prisoners by keeping them for long months in solitary confinement, by clever questioning and, if necessary, by torture. Nobody was too high or too low to be caught, and the Inquisition never let go until the prisoner had confessed and been punished, or been able to convince the Inquisitors that he was in every way a good Catholic.

Therefore the Inquisition was feared, and nobody feared it more than foreign sailors, especially those from Protestant

left: Francisco Ximenes de Cisneros; born 1436, friar 1484, confessor to queen 1492, archbishop of Toledo 1495, founded University of Alcala 1500. Grand Inquisitor 1507. Regent of Castile 1516, died 1517. Bas-relief portrait made between 1513 and 1519 by Felipe Vigarny.

countries like England. To be arrested in a Spanish port, or to be captured as a pirate or smuggler by the king of Spain's forces, might mean being handed over to the Inquisition. So it is easy to imagine how stories of the cruelty of the Inquisition grew and grew, until the horrors of the torture-chambers of the Inquisition have become a legend.

In fact, the Inquisition was less harsh to its prisoners than most courts and governments of sixteenth-century Europe. The only tortures allowed were those which would do no permanent damage to the prisoner. A doctor had to be present. Torture could only be applied once to any prisoner – though this rule was sometimes twisted – and confessions made under torture had to be confirmed by the prisoner afterwards. The punishments which followed an *auto-de-fé* were not specially cruel, either. Throughout most of its history the Inquisition usually burnt people either after they had already been strangled, or else in effigy; comparatively few were burnt alive. Whatever the stories about it, the Inquisition was not cruel, as things were judged in the sixteenth century. What was really frightening about the Inquisition was its thoroughness and success.

Besides catching people who had already 'gone wrong' in religion, the Inquisition tried to protect Spaniards from the danger of picking up ideas which might mislead them. After the middle of the sixteenth century, Spaniards were not allowed to study at foreign universities. There was a strict check on books being brought into the country, for the Inquisition issued lists of books which must not be read in Spain. Smuggling forbidden books could carry the death penalty, and Inquisitors inspected shops, libraries and people's homes to make sure that none had slipped through. This censorship was not the only one in Europe, for many governments tried to suppress books or pamphlets which they did not like, but it was the most thorough.

So Spain became a kingdom where neither Lutheran nor Calvinist ideas had any chance of taking root. If it were to come to fighting, Spaniards would be proud to be the champions of the Catholic Church.

Auto-de-fé at Valladolid, Trinity Sunday, 29 May 1559. This was a famous auto, for a group of Protestants had been found in the heart of Spain itself; on this day 30 were sentenced, of whom 14 were burnt. The prisoners are shown being led from their prison, past balconies where their sentences are announced. All except one yielded at last to the words of the monks and gentlemen escorting them, and died Catholics. This print was made in Germany shortly afterwards.

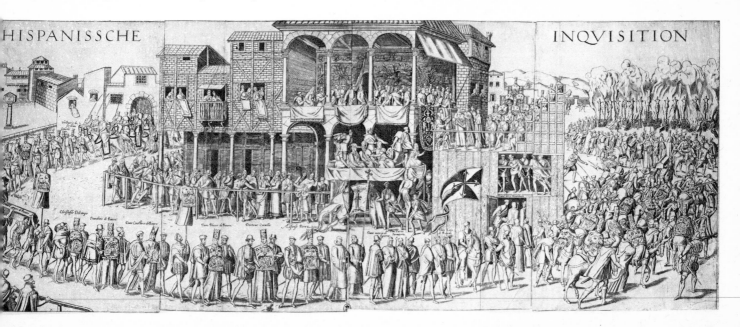

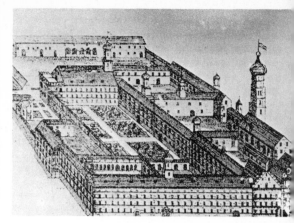

The Jesuits

It was a Spanish ex-soldier, Ignatius de Loyola, who founded the Society of Jesus. In 1521, while recovering from a serious wound, he began to think about religion, and determined to give the rest of his life to the service of God.

First, he needed to pray, to try to know God and find out the best way to serve Him. He went as a pilgrim to the shrine of Montserrat, worked in a hospital at Manresa, nearby, and lived as a hermit in a cave. All the time he was trying to strengthen his spirit, by thinking about God. Some people try to strengthen their bodies by exercising them regularly. Ignatius Loyola tried to do the same for his mind and spirit, and made up a book called *Spiritual Exercises*. This book became, like Calvin's *Institutes*, one of the most powerful books of the sixteenth century.

Naturally, he thought of going to the Holy Land, to try to convert the Muslims and bring Christianity back to Jerusalem. The strong likelihood that he would be killed was not important. But it was important that he should train himself properly for the task. He knew that he was ignorant. He went first to school, learning with the children. Then he went to the University of Paris, where he studied for seven years. A few of the other students learned of his intentions, and decided to join him. On 15 August 1534, seven friends swore that they would devote their lives to missionary work in the Holy Land; if this were to prove impossible for any reason, they would place themselves entirely at the disposal of the Pope, for whatever work he wished them to do. As it happened, they were prevented from sailing to Palestine, so they offered themselves to the Pope. Soon this tiny Society of Jesus grew into a very powerful religious order.

The Jesuits, as they were also called, worked on two main principles. You have seen both of them in Loyola. One was strict military discipline, the other education. A Jesuit had to be able to suppress his own feelings and ideas until they did not seem to exist, and he had 'corpse-like' obedience to his superiors. These in turn must obey their superior officers, right up to the General of the Order, and he obeyed only the Pope. Recruits were given a long, hard training, with difficult and unpleasant tasks to test their obedience. But there had to be nothing 'corpse-like' about a Jesuit's brain. He had to be highly intelligent and well educated. Only the best men were good enough for the Society of Jesus. And the best men came, answering the challenge of these exacting standards and harsh conditions, glad to be in an order which demanded so much of its members.

With amazing speed the Society of Jesus grew in numbers, wealth and power. Protestants came to hate them with special loathing. They said that Jesuits would stoop to any methods. They were dishonest, with a special trick of twisting words and arguments cunningly to prove that whatever they wanted was right. ('Jesuitical' still means 'crafty' or 'deceitful' in English dictionaries.) They encouraged the murder of Protestant leaders. They were a sinister network of spies. Were these charges true?

It was true that the Jesuits were very clever arguers, both in speaking and writing; what one side regards as cleverness often looks like craftiness to the other. It was true that Jesuits went in disguise to Protestant countries, secretly urging and helping people to remain Catholics. If they were caught in England during the reign of Elizabeth I, they were hanged, drawn and quartered. It is true that some of them became the advisers of Catholic kings, and may have made them harder against Protestants. It is difficult to say whether they encouraged murder or not. In the sixteenth century, and at other times, good men have taught that it is right to kill a tyrant, or a usurper, or a rebel, for such men would certainly be condemned to death if they could be brought to trial. Philip II of Spain had openly put a price on the head of William of Orange, as a rebel, and paid it to the killer's family.

In the long run it may have been none of these dreaded activities of the Jesuits, real or imaginary, but their schools which did most to strengthen their Church. They were said to believe that once they had educated a boy, he would always remain theirs. At any rate, the boys who attended their schools had a first-class education all round, and at the same time were being taught to understand their religion. The Jesuits believed in hard work and thoroughness. A teacher had to study for seventeen years before they considered him to be fully qualified. Pupils were tested and examined frequently, and encouraged to compete for marks. Jesuit schools had the reputation of being the best in Catholic Europe.

Besides all this work in Europe, the Jesuits were brave and skilful missionaries in Asia and America, but that is another story. Their importance in Reformation Europe was that, in the mounting struggle between the Catholic Church and the reformed churches, the Pope now had a force of loyal agents of the very highest ability.

The Entry of St Ignatius into Heaven, painted on the ceiling of the Church of St Ignatius, Rome, in the early 1690s by Andrea Pozzo, himself a Jesuit lay-brother as well as a great artist.

Trent and the Counter-Reformation

In the 1520s, as it became clear that Martin Luther's movement was something that the Church had to take very seriously indeed, it seemed to many Catholics that the Pope ought to call a General Council of the Church. This would bring together bishops and learned men from all parts of western Christendom. They might be able to suggest some way of bringing the Lutheran revolt to an end. Even if this did mean taking notice of some of the things Luther had said about the Church, it would be worth it to bring everybody back inside the same Church once more. The Emperor Charles V thought so.

Yet it was not until 1545 that a General Council met, at Trent, on the borders of Italy and Austria. The main reason for the delay was that the Popes of the early sixteenth century had been more afraid of what a Council might do to them than they were of the Lutherans. Only a hundred years before, soon after the Great Schism, the Council of Basel had tried to take over much of the Pope's power. Now, when many Catholics were saying that the faults of the Church were partly to blame for Luther's outbursts, and that there would have been fewer faults if the Popes had done their duty, you can understand that the Popes had some reason to be nervous.

However, when the Council ended, after several interruptions, in 1563, the Pope's position was stronger than it had been for centuries.

The Council had found that there were two sets of faults in the Church. First, there had been slackness and corruption, which had disgusted many people and made them follow Luther or Calvin. The Council tried many ways of stopping such faults. Bishops were given more powers to deal with the priests and monks in their areas. Strict orders were given that only good, well-qualified men should be made priests. New colleges were set up, called seminaries, specially to educate priests.

Second, the council found that many of the beliefs of the Church had never been very clearly stated. People had not known exactly what they ought to think – until men like Luther and Calvin had told them. Now the Council tried to lay down much more clearly and exactly what the beliefs of the Church were.

All through the Council the Jesuits had been working hard, always arguing against giving way to the Lutherans or Calvinists in anything, and for rallying round the Pope. By the end of the Council, nearly all the members had come round to thinking that the Church really did need to be led by Popes who had full authority to give orders to everybody. So the Council handed over all its decisions to the Pope, for him to enforce them or not, as he saw fit. The Council had not only removed many of the faults of the Church and made it easier for Catholics to know what they believed; it had also decided that there would be no more attempts to challenge the leadership of the Pope. Fortunately, the Popes of the later sixteenth century were men who were well able to give the good example and devoted work which the Church had needed for so long.

The Reformation had brought about the Counter-Reformation. The Catholic Church had been shocked and shaken, and had now pulled itself together. There was new energy, new confidence. Soon there was a new style of church-building to match: the Baroque style. Compare this with the Puritan church on page 60. You can see in the buildings the head-on collision between the two religions. Challenge had been met by challenge, and the Catholic Church was now ready to try to win back the millions of people it had lost to the Reformed churches.

right: Baroque churches in three Catholic countries. The rich, crowded, elaborate decoration may create an impression of splendour, energy and confidence.

top: Monastic church of Stams, Tyrol; to the original medieval church the ceiling was added between 1601 and 1615, and the other decoration about 1730.

bottom left: Pilgrimage church of Hafnerberg, Lower Austria; pulpit made in 1745.

bottom centre: Church of Jesus, Rome; altar of St Ignatius, made about 1685 by Andrea Pozzo.

bottom right: Carthusian church, Granada, built between 1730 and 1747.

The Wars of Religion

History is full of wars, and you have already found that the century of the Renaissance and Reformation had its fair share. The great wars of the earlier part of the century had nothing to do with religion. The great wars which came later, between about 1580 and 1660, are often known as the Wars of Religion. It is true that people of different religions fought against one another – there have been many 'Holy Wars' and 'Crusades' in history – but it is a bad mistake to think that religion was the only reason for these wars. It may not even have been the main one. You can argue about the relative importance of the reasons behind these wars.

Philip of Spain

Though he had not been given the whole of the possessions of his father, the Emperor Charles V, Philip II of Spain was very much the most important king in Europe, especially after he inherited Portugal and the Portuguese Empire in 1580. He was the central figure in the first series of religious wars, and nobody has ever doubted that he was a very sincere, devoted Catholic, and that he wanted to see Protestantism defeated and destroyed. But was that why he got involved in wars?

Philip, like his father, had many things to worry about in different places, without going out of his way to start anything else. The Dutch rose against him (page 63) and this was partly about religion; but the rebels also objected to the heavy taxes, their nobles were afraid that Philip was going to take away some of their powers and privileges, and they simply did not like being ruled by Spaniards. Philip sent soldiers to help the Catholics in the wars in France (page 62), but he did not intervene very strongly until the Catholic leaders were so weak that they had to do exactly as he said, and offered the crown of France

left: The defeat of the Spanish Armada, July 1588. This painting is thought to have been made soon afterwards as a design for a tapestry, and gives no real idea of battle, but shows the types of ships in the most decorative way. In the foreground a Spanish galleass, flying papal as well as royal arms, is between two English galleons, one displaying royal arms on its foresail.

to his daughter. Everyone has heard how Philip tried to invade England in 1588, with the Armada; but he had left Elizabeth in peace for thirty years, and only fought because there was no other way of stopping English help to the Dutch rebels, and the raids of English sailors on his colonies and shipping. Besides, Mary Queen of Scots, beheaded in 1587, had left her claim to the English crown to Philip.

On the whole, those wars were drawn. The map of Europe was very much the same in, say, 1610 as it had been in 1580, both religious and political. There was one big change which was taking place. Spain was becoming poorer, and the Netherlands richer through trade. But this was not obvious to everybody, and Spain still seemed to be the greatest military power in Europe.

We should not forget that Philip II had also fought the Turks in the Mediterranean, where a Spanish and Italian fleet had won the great naval victory of Lepanto in 1571. This war was another religious war, but it was also to defend his shores and ships against Muslim attacks.

Philip II; born 1527, king of Spain 1556, died 1598. Portrait by an unidentified artist, about 1580.

Lepanto, 7 October 1571, shown in a contemporary painting. With about 500 galleys engaged, this may have been the greatest naval battle of all time. The red galleys with white crosses belong to the Knights of St John, famous for their heroic repulse of a mighty Turkish attack on their base at Malta six years earlier.

The Thirty Years' War

The last big religious war broke out in 1618, twenty years after the death of Philip II. It arose from quite a small dispute inside the Holy Roman Empire, when the Protestants in Bohemia tried to appoint a Protestant as their king, instead of the emperor, who was a Catholic. The war spread across the empire, with German Catholic and Protestant states gradually joining in. Then it spread further. Spain sent soldiers to help the emperor (both the king of Spain and the emperor were members of the Habsburg family) and the Catholics began to win. Then Sweden came in, under her soldier-king, Gustavus Adolphus, and the Protestants won great victories. But in one of those battles Gustavus was killed, and the Catholics started to win again. It looked as though the Catholic side, led by the Habsburgs, might conquer the whole of Germany.

France was a Catholic country. Louis XIII allowed Cardinal Richelieu (page 4) to direct his government. Because he was a cardinal, you might have expected Richelieu to support the Catholics, especially when you learn that he had taken away from the French Protestants the fortresses which Henry IV had given them (page 62). But Richelieu was the leader of France, and he had no intention of letting the Habsburgs win the war in Germany. If they won, the emperor and the king of Spain, between them, might be masters of all Europe. So the cardinal sent his armies into the war on the *Protestant* side.

In 1648 the Peace of Westphalia was signed, ending the war in Germany. For eleven more years France and Spain carried on their own fight, and then signed the Treaty of the Pyrenees. The map shows the lands which changed rulers in those treaties. They may not seem very large, but some were important. Notice how Sweden got control of the mouths of the principal German rivers. After this, Sweden was mistress of the Baltic Sea.

As for France and Spain, their positions had been reversed. Spain had at last been beaten, and collapsed; the strain of the past 150 years, during which Spain had tried to dominate Europe and hold an empire which stretched all the way round the world, had finally ruined the country. Spain was exhausted, bankrupt, and from now on she was not considered very seriously by the other countries in Europe. For the next two centuries France was to be the leading power in Europe.

left: Gustavus Adolphus and his army, proud and strong, march into Frankfurt-on-Main while the city's guns fire a salute, 1631. Copper-engraving by Matthaeus Merian the elder.

right: In 1633 the French engraver Jacques Callot published a collection of etchings entitled *The Miseries and Calamities of War*. Here we see soldiers, crippled and destitute, seeking charity at a hospital.

Germany had been the battle-ground for the armies of all Europe for thirty years, and had suffered dreadful losses. Historians argue just how bad they were; it used to be said that it took Germany a full century to recover, but that sort of saying does not really tell us much: how can you measure recovery? Anyway, the Holy Roman Emperor had tried to assert himself and had failed. Germany was to remain divided into hundreds of small states.

But what of religion?

After all that fighting, not one country had changed its religion. Had the wars been worth fighting? Or had they ever been about religion, really?

Now the so-called religious wars were ended. Partly this may have been because neither side thought that it could ever succeed completely. Partly it was because most of the kings and statesmen of Europe were now thinking that religion was one thing, politics another, and it was a mistake to confuse the two, at least in international affairs. Some people were even thinking that a king need not bother about making all his people belong to his own religion, as long as they were loyal subjects. It was still to be a long time before most governments in Europe were to allow freedom of religion to their people, but at least Protestants and Catholics had now learnt that they could not destroy each other's Churches.

Central Europe after the Wars of Religion
(Peace of Westphalia, 1648
Peace of the Pyrenees 1659)

Lands held by King of France — Gains 1648–59
Lands held by King of Sweden — Gains 1648–60
Lands held by King of Spain
Land held by Austrian Habsburgs
Boundary of Holy Roman Empire (note shrinking)

3. THE ENGLISH REVOLUTION

Elizabeth and her people

Elizabeth I; born 1533, queen 1558, died 1603. Miniature painted by Nicholas Hilliard in 1572; the original is only 2 inches (5 cm) high.

Gloriana

Everyone knows how splendid Elizabethan England was: the glittering court, the poets and playwrights and musicians, the sea-dogs who sailed round the world and defeated the Spanish Armada, the stately great houses of the lords and ladies, the cosy half-timbered dwellings of the yeoman farmers and comfortable merchants. Even the underworld of gamblers and cheats, robbers and cut-purses, vagabonds and beggars, seems to have an air of glamour.

That is only one side of the picture, of course, for there was much fear, poverty, savagery and defeat in Elizabethan England. All the same, the good side was there. It was true enough. And at the centre of it was the queen herself. She was a woman of brilliant ability, and one of her greatest gifts was the power to inspire love and fear at the same time among her people. It was the fashion for courtiers and poets to pay her extravagant compliments, to write flattering verses, to sing of the grace and wisdom and beauty and power of 'Gloriana, the Virgin Queen'. The queen was pleased to accept such praise, not because she was silly enough to swallow it all, but because she knew that a touch of splendour and romance helped to build up the idea that the queen was not like ordinary people. This made her position stronger.

Her reputation became even greater after her death. Her successor was a Scotsman, King James I of England and VI of Scotland, which did not make him popular to begin with. Then, though learned and well-meaning, he was undignified (he slobbered and was easily frightened), tactless, and had an unfortunate way of annoying and misjudging people. With such a man on the throne, Englishmen began to look back to the reign of Elizabeth as if it had been a golden age.

The problem of religion

After the death of Henry VIII in 1547 there was the boy-king, Edward VI. He and his advisers were firmly Protestant, and ordered many changes in the Church of England to make it more Protestant. After six years Edward died, and the throne went to Queen Mary, who was firmly Catholic. She brought the Church back to obeying the Pope. Many Protestants were burnt at the stake, which earned for her the nickname of 'Bloody Mary'. She died after five years on the throne.

When Elizabeth came to the throne next, in 1558, she was therefore faced by a complete mix-up, with many of her people Protestant, many of them Catholic, and probably most of them confused and vague. One thing was certain. Elizabeth herself could not be a Catholic, for she was the daughter of Anne Boleyn. Catholics argued that Anne had never been properly married to Henry VIII, which meant that Elizabeth was illegitimate, which meant that she could not inherit the throne. On the other hand, Elizabeth had no desire to offend the many Catholics in England, and she did not want to be attacked by Catholic kings from abroad. It was tricky.

Elizabeth's solution was this. She made the Church of England Protestant once more. But she did not call herself 'Head' of the Church, only 'Governor'; she kept bishops and a great amount of ceremonial; and she had some beliefs written down in the Prayer Book so vaguely that people could put either a Catholic or a Protestant meaning to them, whichever they preferred. So Elizabeth tried to make it easy for all of her people to come to the Church of England every Sunday without feeling that they were in the wrong church. It was clever and it appeared to work. Gradually most people seem to have settled down in Elizabeth's Church of England.

But – it was a big BUT – the Puritans in England were not satisfied. They said that the Church of England was too much like the Church of Rome. They were loyal to Elizabeth herself, and this was only partly because, for many years, all the other likely claimants to the English throne were Catholics. Elizabeth tried to keep the Puritans down. One of them, for example, had his right hand cut off for writing a pamphlet against one of the queen's policies. (He was loyal though; as soon as he had lost one hand, he took off his hat with the other and shouted, 'God save the Queen!') In Parliament some of the M.P.s were Puritans, and sometimes insisted on offering the queen advice that she did not want. She sent such men to cool off for a year or two in the Tower of London. So Elizabeth made sure that everybody knew who was boss in England. But she could not prevent more and more people, including wealthy people, from preferring Puritanism to her Church of England.

far left: Edward VI; born 1537, king 1547, died 1553. Portrait painted about 1546.

left: Mary I; born 1516, queen 1553, married Philip of Spain 1554, died 1558. Portrait probably painted during her reign.

The problem of money

Though she spent as little as she possibly could, even on her navy, and though she insisted on a share of the profits from anybody who could be 'squeezed', from bishops to pirates, Elizabeth was short of money. Parliament, for all its loyalty, never managed to vote her enough.

One method which the queen tried to get over the money shortage was monopolies. It worked like this. Suppose she rewarded a courtier by giving him the monopoly of wine in Kent, this meant that he was the only person in the whole of Kent who was allowed to sell wine. So all the wine-sellers would have to get permission from the monopolist, as the man with the monopoly was called, and they would have to pay for it. Thus the queen gave money to her courtier without any cost to herself. But the wine-sellers would either have to bear the cost themselves, or charge their customers more.

There were many complaints about monopolies. At last, not very long before she died, the queen had to promise Parliament not to grant any more monopolies. She did it so gracefully that it would have been easy for anyone not to have noticed that in fact it was a surrender. Parliament had made the queen promise to do what it wanted.

The problem of Parliament

If you think back to the reign of the first Tudor king, Henry VII, Elizabeth's grandfather, you will remember that the 'new men' of the middle class had been only too pleased to be made the king's helpers. In a hundred years, though, they had become used to doing important jobs, and were beginning to think of themselves as full partners in ruling the country.

If you think back to Elizabeth's father, Henry VIII, you may remember how he used Parliament to pass his Acts against the Pope. Though it was not his intention, this encouraged Parliament to think of itself as the king's partner.

By the end of her reign Elizabeth, last of the Tudors, was needing all her skill to keep Parliament in its place.

In the Tudor century, Parliament's attitude had changed from being willing to let the king direct anything to wanting a real share in deciding which road the government should follow.

A 'new' family which rose to greatness in the Tudor century.

1st generation: Edmund Dudley, taxgatherer for Henry VII; beheaded 1510.

2nd generation: son John, general and admiral for Henry VIII, Protector of Edward VI; made himself duke of Northumberland and tried to make daughter-in-law, Jane Grey, queen; beheaded 1553 (*left:* detail of a portrait).

3rd generation: son Robert, earl of Leicester, favourite and nearly husband of Elizabeth I; died 1588 (*left, centre*).

4th generation: stepson Robert Devereux, earl of Essex, favourite of Elizabeth I in her old age; beheaded 1601 (*left:* detail of a portrait).

5th generation: son Robert was general of the Parliamentary army in the Civil War.

Helping the king to govern —
1500
1600
need not always mean the same thing.

below: James I and VI; born 1566, king of Scotland 1567, king of Britain 1603, died 1625. Painted in his robes of state, 1621, by Daniel Mytens.

Towards civil war

The Divine Right of Kings

As you saw on page 76, James I, the first of the Stuart family to reign over England, seemed a poor thing compared with Elizabeth. He was not a fool. He had done well in Scotland, in difficult conditions. Perhaps he made the mistake of thinking that England, a richer and more orderly land, would be easier to handle, and he may have found it hard to learn that he would need different methods with this different people. One great mistake was the way he believed in the Divine Right of Kings.

There was nothing new in the idea that kings had been appointed by God himself in order to look after their peoples. During the Middle Ages some kings and emperors had used this argument in their quarrels with bishops or Popes. Now that kings had become so much stronger, and churches depended so much on them, it was very easy for a king to believe it. If God had appointed the king, disobedience to the king was disobedience to God. Even if a king were to behave badly, he must not be resisted; it was for God to punish him, in His own time. Several kings in several lands, and their followers, believed this. Often it made the king take his duties very seriously, because he felt that God had given him such great responsibility.

James I and, after his death in 1625, his son Charles I believed in Divine Right. They expected Parliament to believe the same. From what you know of the way the English Parliament had been behaving in the reign of Elizabeth, you will understand that king and Parliament were soon at cross-purposes. To make matters worse, more Puritans were becoming M.P.s, while James and Charles believed very firmly in the Church of England, and there was hatred between the Church of England bishops and the Puritans who accused them of being no better than Catholics. There were further wrangles between king and Parliament about money. Feelings became so strained that whenever the king called a Parliament there was quarrelling about one thing or another. It seemed that the king and most M.P.s had reached the stage where they disagreed about everything, from amusements to the conduct of war.

King without Parliament

In 1629 Charles I decided that, even though it meant giving up all hope of the taxes which only Parliament could vote him, he was going to try to rule without the 'help' of Parliament. For eleven years he managed quite well. He raised money by charging fees and fines from laws that people had forgotten about. When he needed warships, he found an old tax called Ship Money. It was not popular with some of the men who had to pay, but it was legal.

Then Charles made a grave mistake. In 1637 he tried to make the Scottish Presbyterians use a new Prayer Book, like that of the Church of England. The Scots refused. The king tried again. The Scots formed an army, and many of them were skilled soldiers who had been mercenaries in the Thirty Years' War under Gustavus Adolphus. Charles had no army, and the rabble he hastily raised was useless. In 1640 the Scots occupied Northumberland and Durham, and threatened to advance further south unless they were paid £850 a day (that would be worth twenty or thirty times as much nowadays). Charles could only find the money in one way. He had to call Parliament.

below: Charles I; born 1600, king of Britain 1625, beheaded 1649. Portrait in the style of Sir Anthony van Dyck. Charles was a connoisseur and patron of art, and knighted the painter.

below: William Laud; born 1573, archbishop of Canterbury 1633, beheaded 1645. Part of a portrait, in the style of Van Dyck. Laud believed in Divine Right and encouraged ceremony in church services; Puritans detested him.

The fighting starts

Two years later, in 1642, the English Civil War began. On one side was the king, with most of the Lords and some of the members of the House of Commons. On the other side were most of the House of Commons, and some of the Lords. All the same, it is fair to say that the war was between those who thought that the king should really rule the country, and those who thought that Parliament should have the last word. So the war was about politics, about how England should be ruled.

It was also about religion, because the Puritans were for Parliament, while Church of England people naturally were for the king. Catholics, too, were for the king, as they knew that the Puritans disliked them much more than the Church of England did.

The war may have been brought about by many other things. As you know, it was partly about money, because the king wanted it and Parliament insisted on controlling it. The war may also have been caused by certain people wanting power; perhaps John Pym and a few more of the leading M.P.s, or perhaps a whole class of wealthy men, city merchants and country gentlemen, who felt that they ought to run England. Historians argue over what the war was mainly about, and in fact it was about many things.

Hardly anybody seems to have *wanted* war. You often see maps showing which parts of the country were for king or for Parliament when the war started. These maps are correct, but they may mislead anybody who does not stop to ask what being 'for' king or Parliament meant. Usually, it meant that one or two important men in the district were on that side, and they decided what their town or county would do. What is certain is that most Englishmen did not want to fight at all. It is important to remember that.

It would need a long account of what happened in the three years, 1640–1–2, to show how both sides gradually got themselves into such a position that they could not do anything but fight. To explain very briefly, at first the king had given way completely to the leaders of the House of Commons. He had promised not to raise any more money without their agreement; had abolished those courts which had helped him, like the Court of Star Chamber; had promised never again to try to go for a long time without Parliament rule, and not to dis-

miss this Parliament without its own consent (this Parliament of 1640 was to be called the Long Parliament, for it was not properly dissolved for twenty years). Charles had even agreed to the execution of his best minister, Strafford.

But, after making the king do all this, would Pym and his friends ever dare let him rule the country again? Would they dare to go home now, and risk the king's trying to take revenge? They did not. Instead, they went further, and tried to make the Church of England become Presbyterian.

By now, many men who had first supported the Parliamentary leaders thought they had gone too far, and were turning to the king. Then there arose the crucial question of the army. A revolt had broken out in Ireland, where the Irish Catholics were killing many of the English and Scottish Protestants who had settled in Ireland and taken the best land. An army was needed to put down the Irish. Everybody agreed about that. But who would command it? Neither side dared let the other have an army.

So both sides sent out orders to the counties that soldiers should be enlisted. The result was two armies, one commanded by the king, the other by Parliament. The king raised his standard at Nottingham on 22 August 1642.

The opening moves 1642

Territory held at the end of each year:
by Parliament   by the King

How Parliament won

As everybody knows, Parliament won the war. Since there is no space in this book to go into the story of the battles and campaigns, we must stick to the most important task, to find out how and why the war went thus.

By the end of 1643 the war had been going on long enough for each side to realise that it had better obtain help if it were to have a good chance of beating the other decisively. So each side looked beyond England. Naturally, the Parliamentary leaders looked to their fellow-Presbyterians in Scotland, whose army had been paid off after its stay in northern England in 1640, but who had proved their military value. This left the king only Ireland to look to, because neither side was foolish enough to think seriously of seeking aid from outside Britain. There were English soldiers still in Ireland, facing the Irish rebels.

Charles had to make a treaty with the Irish before it was safe to bring the soldiers back, and this treaty harmed his reputation in England. The Irish were hated; English Protestants thought of them as murderous savages, hardly human at all, for there had been horrible stories of cruelty. Anyway, Charles received little help, because the soldiers he brought from Ireland were defeated and mostly captured at Nantwich soon after they landed.

On the other hand, Parliament was greatly assisted by the Scots. They made it possible for the Parliamentary army to wipe out the king's army in the north, at the battle of Marston Moor, in 1644. Now that Parliament held the north, the military map looked grim for the king.

There was still a chance that the king might recover. The Royalists were often better fighters than the Parliamentarians,

The Royalist drive on London 1643

⇐ Royalist move
◀ Parliamentary move

Arrows thus = = = indicate moves that were intended but not achieved.

Newcastle

York

Hull

Nottingham

Leicester

Huntingdon

Gloucester

OXFORD

Bristol

LONDON

Plymouth

Towns underlined held out successfully for Parliament

Help for both sides 1644

FROM SCOTLAND

Newcastle

Marston Moor 2 July

York

Hull

FROM IRELAND

Nottingham

x Nantwich 25 Jan.

Leicester

Huntingdon

x Naseby 14 June 1645

Gloucester

OXFORD

LONDON

Bristol

Plymouth

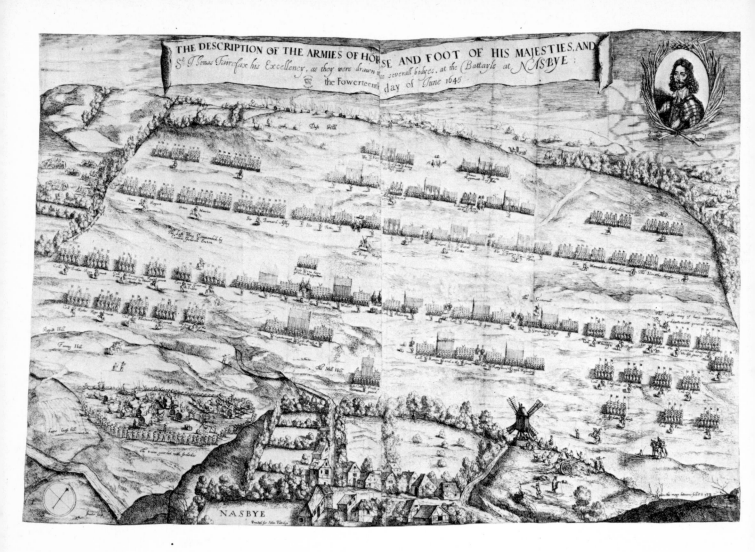

The armies drawn up before the battle of Naseby. The New Model Army is in the foreground. The separate regiments can easily be seen, infantry in the centre and cavalry on the wings. Each infantry regiment consists of one-third pikemen, in the middle and two-thirds musketeers, on each side. The engraving, by Robert Streeter, comes from Joshua Sprigge's *Anglia Rediviva*, published in London, 1647.

and this was especially true of their cavalry. You can see from this print how important the cavalry were in Civil War battles. The big blocks of infantry, with their eighteen-foot pikes and clumsy matchlock muskets, were solid and steady, but very slow. While the infantry were pushing at each other in the centre of the battlefield, the cavalry would win or lose their own fight much more quickly. So one army would be left with only infantry, to struggle against both infantry and cavalry, and there could be only one end to that sort of unequal fight. Therefore it was cavalry which decided the battles.

The Royalist horsemen were led by the king's German nephew, Prince Rupert, who had learnt some lessons in the Thirty Years' War. He let his men charge headlong, scattering the enemy with the shock. There were high-spirited young men in Rupert's cavalry who had been brought up as horsemen, who were used to hunting and who were quite sure that they could chase any number of low-born 'Roundheads'. So they did. But there was one bad fault. They went on chasing the enemy for miles, forgetting about the rest of the battle, which might not be going so well for their side. They needed more discipline.

Discipline   Enthusiasm

A well-equipped cavalryman would wear a buff-coat (stout leather, yellowed in the tanning) breastplate and backplate, lobster-tailed helmet with ear-flaps and sliding faceguard, and sometimes a plate to protect his bridle arm. He would carry a broadsword on waist or shoulder belt, and pistols or a light musket or arquebus. The equipment shown here belonged to Colonel Popham's troop in the Parliamentary army. Pikemen did not wear the stiff, cumbersome buff-coat, but sometimes had tassets to protect their thighs and gorgets at the neck. The helmet relied on a wide brim to give protection without impeding vision or movement. Musketeers, using a weapon so heavy that it needed a fork-shaped support, usually wore no armour.

Discipline was the answer which the Parliamentary army eventually worked out. Oliver Cromwell, a country gentleman from Huntingdon, had raised a regiment of cavalry. He trained them carefully, saw that they were well armed and paid, and insisted that they should all be Puritans, who knew what they were fighting for. Above all, he made sure that they obeyed strict discipline. Cromwell was nicknamed 'Ironsides' by Prince Rupert himself, it is said, and the nickname stuck to his soldiers. These men were a match for the dashing Cavaliers.

Parliament decided that it needed a whole army of men like Cromwell's, properly trained and paid and armed and disciplined. So they set up the New Model Army. It was the first regular professional army in Britain since the Roman army had left, and its uniform was the red coat which the British army kept for three centuries.

The New Model Army won the war for Parliament. It was not the only reason why Parliament won, as you have seen. And one more reason was that Parliament held the sea. The navy had mostly taken Parliament's side, so the big ports which Parliament held could carry on with their trade while the king found it difficult to ship in supplies and arms from abroad. The Royalists were soon desperately short of money.

In 1645, after losing the battle of Naseby, the king had little chance of winning the war. Early in 1646 he realised this. But he might still win the peace. He gave himself up – to the Scottish army, not to Parliament. He was going to try to make the winners fall out.

The army takes over

The winners were in a rather awkward position, because they needed the king. They had not been trying to get rid of him, only to force him to rule the way they wanted. So, though the king knew that he would have to give way on some things, he was still king, and nobody denied it.

He tried to play off the Scots against the English Parliament, but it did not work. The Scots did not want to have any more trouble, and handed him over to Parliament as soon as they had been given the pay which had been promised when they had first agreed to help Parliament. Besides, most of Parliament were Presbyterians, like the Scots, and they had agreed to make England Presbyterian, too.

But now something quite unforeseen happened. The New Model Army began to act on its own, instead of just doing what Parliament commanded. The army was beginning to distrust Parliament. The reasons may sound familiar: money, religion, the struggle for power.

MONEY. Parliament may have been much richer than the king, but by now it was very short of money, and was months behind with the soldiers' pay. When it told many of the soldiers that they were no longer needed, that they could go home, that they would be given their back pay later, the soldiers were suspicious. They refused to go until they had been paid.

RELIGION. The soldiers were Puritans. But most of them had become a different sort of Puritan from most of the members of Parliament. They had become Independents, and thought that each congregation of Puritans should be able to worship as it pleased, without having to accept what a consistory or presbytery said. They feared that the Presbyterians were going to try to make them all worship in exactly the same way, with no freedom. The soldiers, including General Cromwell himself, were not going to submit to this. They said that they had fought to be able to pray in the way that they themselves wanted.

During the War   When the War is over

POWER. This is the first time in English history, as far as we can see, that a large body of ordinary people had had the chance to decide how they wanted the country to be run. Wat Tyler's men, three centuries before, had nearly gained control, but there is nothing to make us suppose that they had thought and argued out for themselves what they were going to do. They had been desperate peasants following anyone who gave them hope of better treatment. The men of the New Model Army were very different. They were the strongest force in the country; they were used to working and fighting together; they were used to helping to run their Puritan congregations; some of them were officers, used to taking decisions and giving orders. Many of these men, now that they had a chance, began to show that they held very different ideas from Parliament.

You know that Parliament was not a place for ordinary people. The men who sat there, even most of the men who voted at elections, were middle-class men, many of them quite rich and some of them very rich. This was not good enough for a great number of the soldiers. Some said that all men, and even women, should have a vote. They said that Parliament ought to be newly elected each year, so that it could not forget its duty to the English people. There were even some who thought that wealth should be shared. There were all sorts of ideas being put forward, many of them printed in pamphlets. Every regiment elected 'agitators' to speak for them in councils representing the whole army. This was something that neither the king nor the Parliament wanted.

Most of the important officers did not want it, either. Cromwell and many others were wealthy gentlemen, believing that only people with a certain amount of wealth, who had something to lose and who were able to look after their own possessions, were fit to help to run the country. These officers persuaded the majority of the army to follow them, so the democratic ideas were gradually forgotten.

For several months everything was very confused. The king, Parliament, some of the Scots, and the army under Cromwell were all trying to get their own way, each trying to decide how far the others would help. In 1648 the king seemed to have managed well. He promised to allow Presbyterianism in England, and a Scottish army marched into England to support him. At the same time, Royalists in England and Wales took up arms again. Parliament did nothing. Cromwell and the army felt that they had been betrayed, fought furiously, and against heavy odds won this Second Civil War.

Cromwell and his men had had enough.

Soldiers led by Colonel Pride went to Parliament and dismissed all the Presbyterian M.P.s. The only members left were those who were friendly to the army. There were only about sixty, and they were soon nicknamed 'The Rump'.

The king was put on trial for causing the Second Civil War, and was executed on 30 January 1649.

By 1651 Cromwell had conquered both Scotland and Ireland. Since the Scots were, after all, Puritans, they were treated quite well. You can guess how the Irish were treated.

When the First Civil War began in 1642 Cromwell had been a fairly unimportant M.P., and the army had not existed. Now they ruled the whole of Britain.

below left: The pamphlet is one of the earlier statements published by the army, but it shows that already the soldiers were concerned with more than their back pay. During the next two years the army held many debates about the liberties of Englishmen.

below right: The beheading of Charles I, from a German print of 1649; the Banqueting Hall from which he stepped on to the scaffold still stands in Whitehall.

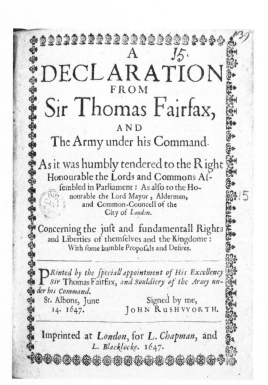

Dictator of England

above: Oliver Cromwell; born 1599, appointed Protector 1653, died 1658. Part of a portrait painted in 1656 in the style of Samuel Cooper. Cromwell is said to have told the painter to show him without flattery as he really was, 'warts and all'.

below: Cromwell's own arms were: sable, a lion rampant argent. When he became Protector this shield was placed upon arms representing the Commonwealth, combining symbols of England, Ireland and, after 1654, Scotland.

There is as much argument over this man as there is over Henry VIII. Some people think of him as an unselfish, tolerant, liberty-loving Christian, whose only desire was to serve God and England. Others think of him as a ruthless, cunning tyrant, who was interested only in power for himself. Oliver Cromwell did and said so much that it is not difficult to find words and deeds which seem to support either opinion. When reading what is said about him here, remember that there is very much more to be read about him, and that many historians would judge him differently.

From 1649 to 1653 Cromwell and the army were supposed to be serving a government known as the Commonwealth, which was mainly made up of members of the Rump Parliament. In 1653 Cromwell took power openly, ruling the Commonwealth of Britain with the title of Protector.

You already know that there were many people who did not like the Protector; you have only to look back at all those whom he and the army had put down, and you can make a list of Cromwell's enemies. Besides, it seems likely that many people had been shocked by the execution of the king, and felt that England was a kingdom, that it was somehow wrong not to have a king. So it looks as though Cromwell began his rule with many more people against him than for him.

It meant that Cromwell would not last long unless he had armed force behind him. But with the support of the army, of course, he was strong enough to rule England as he pleased.

What did he want? Cromwell thought that God had given him the duty of protecting 'God's people', by which Cromwell meant Puritans. So he had to make sure that there was no danger from Catholics, either in Britain or abroad. He tried to make the Church of England Puritan, and many vicars were dismissed and replaced by Puritan ministers. He tried to make the English behave in a more 'godly' way by closing the theatres, stopping many sports and festivities (including Christmas celebrations), and firmly stamping out drunkenness and any sort of disorder. To do this, and especially to watch for any signs of plots against him, he divided England and Wales into eleven districts, each governed by a major-general and his soldiers. Many people detested all this enforced Puritan behaviour, and hated being ordered about by the army. To make matters worse, they had to pay higher and higher taxes to support this army which was bossing them about.

The expense was increased by wars. The Commonwealth had fought the Dutch, mostly because of trade, and the Protectorate fought Spain, over trade and religion. There were victories in both wars, and in the long run England may have profited from both of them by increasing her trade and colonies, but meanwhile it all added to the expense of Cromwell's rule.

So he became less and less popular, which meant that he needed to rely on the army more and more, which made him even less popular, which made him rely on the army even more, which made . . . There was no way out.

It was not that Cromwell was happy at being a military dictator. Next to believing in doing what he thought was God's work, he believed that England should be ruled by a free Parliament. Three times he tried to find a way of working with different sorts of Parliament, trying to get Parliaments which might agree with him by changing the method of electing them. Every time, after starting off in a friendly way, the Protector and his Parliament disagreed, and the real reason behind the disagreement was that Parliament, however it had been elected, tried to persuade Cromwell to give up relying on the army. Since Cromwell knew well enough that this would give his enemies a chance to overthrow him, and Puritanism too, he could never agree.

In 1657 he and his third Parliament tried to get out of the dilemma by going back to something like the old system of government under the king. They brought back an Upper House, like the old House of Lords. Parliament even asked Cromwell to take the title of king, and he nearly did, even though this would have meant that he would have less power than as Protector. He decided against becoming king because many of the officers of the army protested about it, and these were men whom he dared not offend.

So Cromwell had to go on ruling with the army. He failed to make England as a whole become Puritan, and he failed to set up a new system of free Parliaments. Because he was so esteemed and obeyed by his soldiers (and perhaps because many other people, even if they did not agree with him, also had a certain respect for him) he remained firmly in control of Britain until his death on 3 September 1658.

There was nobody strong enough to take his place. His son Richard became Protector, could not make the generals of the army obey him, and resigned. Then the generals could not agree on how the country should be governed. Everybody was fed up. There was a strong feeling that there was only one way of putting a stop to the mess – go back to the old ways, bring back the king.

right: England's naval rivalry with the United Provinces was not affected by changes of government; the First Dutch War was fought by the Commonwealth, the Second and Third by Charles II. The fighting was hard on both sides. Here the flagship *Royal James* is being destroyed by a Dutch fireship at the battle of Solebay, 28 May 1672. It is known that the artists, a father and son both named William van de Velde who were famous marine painters, were present at many sea battles, making sketches from a small boat.

Happy Restoration and Glorious Revolution

The Merry Monarch

Ever since Charles I had died in 1649 his elder son had been calling himself Charles II. Now in 1660 it became a reality. He was welcomed back to England by the surviving members of the old Long Parliament, and by nearly everybody else. After the Commonwealth and Protectorate, most Englishmen were only too glad to have a king again.

It may still seem surprising that the army let it happen, but by 1660 the soldiers themselves felt confused and discontented. Their wages were not being paid properly. Their generals were arguing so much that nobody could feel quite sure about obeying their orders. The only regiments to remain a well-disciplined army were those stationed away from the others, in Scotland, under the command of General Monk. When Monk finally decided that nothing would work except the old system of king and Parliament together, he was able

to march his troops to London, protect the M.P.s of the old Long Parliament who had reassembled, and make sure that Charles II was invited to return to England. The rest of the soldiers – partly because Charles had promised them their back pay – did not interfere.

Charles II has been nicknamed 'the Merry Monarch', and with good reason. He was cheerful, witty, fond of a good time and of gay company. Besides, after so many years under Puritan rule, now that the theatres were reopening, for example, and the horses were racing at Newmarket, the feeling that you could enjoy yourself again without being thought a criminal was very strong in England. Charles, with his overdressed courtiers, his funny little spaniels, and his spectacular mistresses, seemed to be the playboy king of a glad nation.

That was how it looked. But gladness would not last for ever, and Charles II was very much more than a playboy. Even from the start, in 1660, though Charles himself was in favour of forgiving and forgetting, there were signs that old quarrels were not over yet. The Cavaliers who had suffered for their loyalty to Charles I – many of them had had their lands confiscated, or had to sell their lands to pay the fines which Cromwell had imposed on them – wanted their own back. The Church of England, too, now that it was once more in charge of England's religion, had Parliament pass several acts: they prevented anyone who would not 'conform' to the services of the Church of England from worshipping according to his own beliefs. Though the acts also hit Catholics, they were mainly aimed against Puritans. Many of these 'Nonconformists', as they came to be called, were fined or imprisoned. One of the most famous of them was John Bunyan, who wrote *The Pilgrim's Progress* during his long years in Bedford jail. All this showed that underneath the cheers and rejoicing, the old feuds were strong.

The first Parliament elected after the Restoration was so full of Royalists that it has been called 'the Cavalier Parliament'. Yet even this Parliament was not able to find the king enough money in taxes for him to run the country, and he had to start thinking of other ways of getting it. One way was to sign a secret treaty with the king of France, promising to

Charles II; born 1630, claimed title of king 1649, began reign effectively 1660, died 1685. Portrait in the style of Sir Peter Lely; by now it was becoming usual to knight court artists.

help him, in return for a good pension. Since the king of France, Louis XIV, was already the strongest king in Europe, believed in the Divine Right of Kings, and was not fond of Protestants, this alarmed many M.P.s when they heard rumours about it. There were many who attended the Church of England so as not to pay fines, but who were Puritans, Nonconformists, at heart. Such men were even more alarmed when Charles's brother James, Duke of York, became a Catholic. This looked terribly dangerous. Charles II, though he had many bastards, had no legitimate children; therefore Catholic James would be the next king, unless something could be done to stop it.

So there gradually formed a body of M.P.s and lords who wanted Parliament to be stronger than the king, who hated and feared Catholics and sympathised with Puritan Nonconformists. They began to call themselves the Country Party, as against the Court Party. Their enemies gave them the same nickname as some Puritan Scottish outlaws – 'Whigs'.

The other group, the Court Party, were for the king, believing the Divine Right idea. They were also strongly for the Church of England, with bishops and ceremonies, what is sometimes called High Church. They detested Nonconformists, and the Whigs said that they were too friendly to Catholics. Their enemies nicknamed them after Irish Catholic outlaws – 'Tories'.

By the 1670s serious trouble was brewing. At last the Whigs, led by Lord Shaftesbury, tried to force Charles to disinherit James. Shaftesbury used every trick he could think of, including spreading panic. He said there was a plot by Catholics to murder the king, take over England, and crush all Protestants. This was called the 'Popish Plot'. Many innocent Catholics were hanged on false evidence, especially because of the tales invented by Titus Oates, who claimed to have learnt the secrets of the Jesuits. But Shaftesbury failed. He was up against Charles II, and Charles turned out to be one of the cleverest politicians who ever sat on an English throne.

To cut a long complicated story very short, Charles was able to hold on for months, then years, always seeming as if he was about to give in to the Whigs. But he never disinherited James. Shaftesbury meanwhile tried to keep the pressure up, with new tales about the wicked Catholics. He thought that he was keeping the panic at boiling point. Charles judged that most people in England were getting tired of it. Charles was

right. He chose his moment, suddenly dissolved Parliament when the Whigs were not prepared – and nothing happened. He arrested some of the chief Whigs, and still nobody stirred. Charles had won. For the last few years of his reign he ruled without Parliament, and there was no trouble anywhere.

England was quiet and loyal. Abroad, Louis XIV had been so alarmed at the prospect of the Whigs, who hated him, getting control of England, that he was glad to pay Charles enough money to keep him comfortable. Money was coming in from customs, too. There had been two more wars against the Dutch, in the 1660s and 1670s, and as a result English sailors and merchants were now enjoying some of the trade which the Dutch used to have. When he died in 1685 Charles II had seemingly recovered all that his father had lost.

This was a period of growing interest in science. The Royal Society was founded in 1662, and one of its early secretaries was Robert Hooke, 1635–1703. Here is a microscope he made, with a replica of his method of focusing light on the subject.

oil reservoir

flame

water-filled globe

glass lens

microscope

The Revolution of 1688

The Stuart family, though they could sometimes be clever at other things, were usually poor politicians. Charles II had been a rare exception. His brother James, now James II, proved to be remarkably inept even for a Stuart. After only three years he was fleeing from England with everybody, even his own soldiers and his own daughters, happy to see the last of him.

He did everything wrong. He put aside laws forbidding Catholics to hold certain important jobs (the correct terms for what he did are 'suspending' the laws, and 'dispensing' with them) and was able to get the judges to declare that he had the power to do this. He began to increase the army. Charles II had kept on some of Cromwell's old regiments, and this had been the beginning of the regular British army. James, though, enlisted many of the dreaded Catholic Irish, and then stationed part of the army near London, as if to warn the Londoners, who had a reputation for being vigorous Protestants, to behave themselves. All this alarmed the Whigs, especially as James had shown himself to be a harsh man by the severity with which he put down a rising led by the duke of Monmouth in south-

west England. The rebels had been defeated at Sedgemoor, the last pitched battle fought on English soil, and many of them had been hunted down and hanged, or sent as slave labour to the plantations in the West Indies.

But the Whigs were not alone in fearing James. Even the Tories did. Tories were loyal to the king, but they also were loyal to the Church of England. Now it looked as though they would have to choose between king and Church. James did not even know who his friends were. When seven Church of England bishops petitioned him to think again about changing the laws against Catholics, he had them put in the Tower of London, and tried for sedition (stirring up disloyalty). Even James's judges found them not guilty. Later, when James had been driven out, most of those bishops remained loyal to him and refused to recognise the next king. Yet James had mistaken them for enemies.

In 1688 some leading Whigs sent a letter to the Netherlands, inviting Prince William of Orange (who was James's nephew) and his wife Mary, who was a daughter of James but a Protestant, to bring an army to England to set the land free. William did. There was no fighting. Everybody deserted James, and the old king slipped away across the Channel, to beg help from Louis XIV.

Since James had gone, William and the Whigs were able to make a deal. William and Mary became king and queen, and William could therefore use Britain in his alliances and wars against his great enemy, Louis XIV of France. In return, he agreed to the Bill of Rights. Some clauses of the Bill are:

'That the pretended power of suspending of laws . . . without the consent of Parliament is illegal.

'That levying of money . . . without consent of Parliament is illegal.

'That the raising or keeping of a Standing army within the kingdom in time of peace unless it be with the consent of Parliament is against law.

'That election of members of Parliament ought to be free.

'That the freedom of speech and debates or proceedings in Parliament ought not to be impeached or questioned in any court or place out of Parliament.

'That for redress of grievances and for the amending strengthening and preserving of the laws Parliaments ought to be held frequently.'

James II; born 1633, king 1685, expelled 1688, died 1701. Painted 1685 by Sir Godfrey Kneller, baronet. The ship and anchor refer to James's successes at sea and at the Admiralty when he was the Duke of York.

In other words, the king had better not try again to do anything which Parliament did not like.

There were other acts to keep the king in order. New Parliaments had to be called triennially which, of course, meant a general election every three years. Judges were not to be interfered with. There was to be no censorship of books and papers (newspapers were just beginning to be widely read). The king must always be a Protestant.

There were two acts which Parliament passed for only one year at a time. These were the Appropriation Act, dealing with government money, and the Mutiny Act, which forbade soldiers to disobey orders. So, if the king were to let more than one year go by without summoning Parliament, he would not legally be able to raise money or to make his troops obey him.

No wonder the victorious Whigs called this the 'Glorious Revolution'.

below: The landing of William of Orange at Brixham, 5 November 1688; a contemporary painting by an unidentified Dutch artist who has made the tower look distinctly un-English. This was the last successful invasion of Britain, and the landing was not opposed.

top right: William III; born 1650, stadholder of United Provinces 1672, married Mary 1677, king of Britain 1689, died 1702. Painted in the style of C. Johnson.

centre: Mary II; born 1662, married William 1677, queen of Britain 1689, died 1694. Painted in the style of W. Wissing.

bottom right: Anne; born 1665, married Prince George of Denmark 1683, queen of Britain 1702, died 1714. Painted in the style of J. Clostermann.

Each of these pictures is a detail of a larger portrait.

The victory of the Whigs

In England and Wales the Revolution was accepted without sign of protest. Indeed, most people seem to have been pleased. The same is true of the Scottish Lowlands; that is, the part of Scotland where most of the people lived and which was, as you know, Presbyterian. But there were two parts of Britain where men fought for James. (Such men became known as Jacobites because the Latin for James is Jacobus.)

One of these areas was the Scottish Highlands. The clans who lived there were different from the Lowlanders in almost every way: they spoke Gaelic instead of English, wore kilts, obeyed their chiefs instead of the ordinary law; and many of them had remained Catholic. An army of Highlanders, led by Lord Dundee, rose for King James, and defeated the government troops in the valley of Killiecrankie. But in the moment of victory Dundee was killed, and then the Highlanders just drifted away home. In 1692 the government made an example of some Macdonalds whose chief was late in swearing loyalty; they were massacred in Glencoe by Campbell soldiers.

There was still support for James and his family in the Highlands, as the Risings of 1715 and 1745 were to prove. But the men who really mattered in Scotland ruled in the Lowlands, and knew that it was best for them to work closely with the rulers of England. In 1707 the Act of Union was passed by both Scottish and English Parliaments. Since then, though Scotland has kept her own laws, there has been only one Parliament for both countries.

In Ireland there was far more support for James. The Irish Catholics knew what to expect from William of Orange and his supporters. At the same time, the Protestants of Northern Ireland, or Ulster, knew what to expect if James recovered Ireland. The Irish, with some help from France, struggled fiercely against William's army. William won the battle of the Boyne on 1 July 1690 (by the New Style Gregorian Calendar, not adopted in Britain until 1752, it was 12 July, still celebrated by the Protestants of Ulster), but the fighting went on until in 1691 a treaty was made at Limerick, promising favourable terms to the Irish. When the Irish had laid down their arms, the treaty was not kept. For the next century Ireland was a land where the Protestant landlords lived well, while the great bulk of the people, the Catholic peasants, existed in poverty.

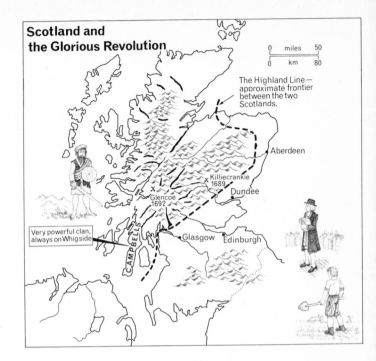

Scotland and the Glorious Revolution

The Highland Line — approximate frontier between the two Scotlands.

Aberdeen

Killiecrankie 1689

Glencoe 1692

Dundee

Very powerful clan, always on Whig side

CAMPBELL

Glasgow   Edinburgh

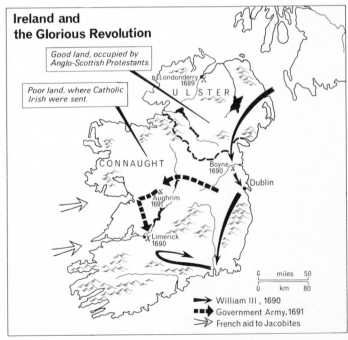

Ireland and the Glorious Revolution

Good land, occupied by Anglo-Scottish Protestants.

Poor land, where Catholic Irish were sent.

Londonderry 1689

ULSTER

CONNAUGHT

Boyne 1690

Dublin

Aughrim 1691

Limerick 1690

→ William III, 1690
▶ Government Army, 1691
⇒ French aid to Jacobites

In England, the Whigs strengthened their grip. There were times when their victory did not seem to be complete. King William did not trust either Whigs or Tories very much; he thought, quite correctly, that most of them would desert him as rapidly as they had deserted James II if anything went wrong. He died without children, and his sister-in-law Anne, the second Protestant daughter of James II, became queen. She began by favouring the Whigs, but tired of them and began to favour Tories. She had no surviving children, either, and after her death the crown was to go – there had been an Act of Parliament about it – to the German Elector George of Hanover. He was a distant relative, but there were no nearer relatives except the Catholic son of James II, a young man who now claimed to be James III since the death of his father in 1701.

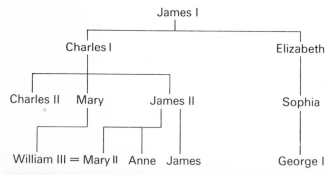

It may all sound complicated when explained briefly, but what it came to was this. In 1714, when Queen Anne was dying, the Tories were faced with a choice. They could back George of Hanover; but he was a long way from the direct line of the royal family, which worried people who thought about kings as the Tories did. Also, it was known that George preferred the Whigs. On the other hand they could back James 'III', who certainly had the best claim. But he was a Catholic, and the Tories were devoted to the Church of England. It really was an impossible position. So they hesitated and wrangled and intrigued until it was too late to do anything. Anne died. George of Hanover was proclaimed King George I, as the existing law required. George knew well that the Whigs were genuinely on his side. Also, he had no great desire to work hard ruling a kingdom in which he was not very interested; he could not express himself easily in English, and preferred to live in Hanover whenever he could. Therefore, George was content to let the Whigs run Britain.

The eighteenth century was to be the great period of Whig Parliamentary control in England. The seventeenth century had been a period of struggle, and the Whig Parliamentarians were the winners. From now on, no British king would try seriously to do without Parliament. The king would keep the laws, only appoint as his ministers men whom Parliament approved, and depend on Parliament for his money.

Parliament was supposed to represent the people of England. But 'people' is a word that can mean almost anything. In this case it certainly did not mean all the people, and it did not mean the great mass of poor and ignorant people. It meant the people with property and good sense, the only people who had a right – so they themselves thought, and the rest seem to have acquiesced – to advise on how the country should be run. These Whigs were prosperous men, their leaders were often great landowners. They did not form one tightly organised party obeying one leader, but were many different groups. Often the group leaders were in the House of Lords, with their friends and relatives – for these groups were frequently based on family connections – sitting in both the House of Lords and the House of Commons. If you remember the way the Greeks named the different types of government a state could have, you will know that the victory of Parliament did not mean democracy; Britain was ruled by an aristocracy, or perhaps an oligarchy.

James III to his supporters, the Pretender to his opponents; born 1688, died 1766. Painted in the style of Belle about 1712 (detail).

George I; born 1660, elector of Hanover 1698, king of Britain 1714, died 1727. Painted in the style of Kneller about 1714 (detail).

despotic monarch

trouble in many parts of Europe. The Thirty Years' War had not only ruined Germany, but had spread misery in other countries where the governments had demanded more and more money and men. The king of Spain was faced by risings in his Italian lands, in Catalonia and in Portugal. Portugal, after a long struggle, broke away from Spain and set up a new royal family, the House of *Braganza*. While Spain, beset by these and other troubles, was sinking from being the chief power in Europe, France was rising to take her place. France, however, was nearly wrecked by peasant revolts and by conspiracies among the nobles. Nevertheless, whether they won or lost the wars between themselves, the kings everywhere were able to overcome all attacks on their power within their states. All over Europe, in the later seventeenth and early eighteenth centuries, kings seemed to be more surely than ever the masters of their states.

It is true that there were one or two republics. Venice was still prosperous, but weak, of no account in the politics of Europe. Switzerland was equally powerless; the Swiss were poor, divided in religion, without a strong central government. The United Provinces, controlled by the merchants of Holland, formed the only important republic in Europe, and even they sometimes accepted the leadership of the prince of Orange.

Britain had become the exception. In Britain the king had become a 'limited' or 'constitutional' monarch. This meant that the king could not do as he wished. 'Constitution' is the name given to all those laws and customs which limit royal power and show how the country ought to be governed. In England the constitution had slowly and painfully taken shape over many years, and still was vague and patchy and left plenty of room for growth. But, such as it was, the king had to abide by it. The despotism of the Tudors had crumbled long ago.

All the same, these Whigs claimed that they guaranteed the liberty of all Britons. It was while they were in power that a popular song was written, declaring: 'Britons never, never, never shall be slaves.' Every man in Britain was protected by the law, could not be punished except after a fair trial by jury. Englishmen, rich and poor alike, boasted that England was the land of liberty.

In most of the kingdoms of Europe, like France or Spain or Sweden, the heirs of the 'new monarchs' were reigning as despots, giving all the orders in Church as well as state. The kings had held, and even increased, the power you saw them gaining at the beginning of this book. It was not that they had had an easy time. The middle of the seventeenth century, about the time of the English Civil War, had been years of

constitutional monarch